MORE PRAISE FOR CASTING FOR BIG I

Andrew Jaffe has used his unique access to the very best thinkers in the agency world, Lee Clow, Jeff Goodby, Keith Reinhard, and others, to create a compelling blueprint for the agency of the future. A fine and thoughtful book.

Sam Hill, President, Helios Consulting

Andrew Jaffe packs a well-informed punch in his premise that agencies have no choice but to reinvent themselves if they are to thrive—never mind survive! He lays down a clear path of step-by-stepping stones for agency leaders to walk on if they hope to realize success in this new century.

Wenda Harris Millard, Chief Sales Officer, Yahoo!, Inc.

This is an essential compendium of the best thinking about reinventing the agency function for the future, assembled by one of the keenest observers of advertising and brand building.

Rick Kurnit, Partner, Frankfurt Kurnit Klein & Selz, PC

Andrew Jaffe's book is a must-read for any corporate advertising manager. In a time of shrinking corporate budgets and increasing calls for accountability, *Casting for Big Ideas* provides a "how-to" guide for getting the most out of the agency relationship.

Krista Pilot, Manager,
Corporate Advertising, United Technologies

CASTING FOR
BIG
IDEAS

Adweek Books and Brandweek Books are designed to present interesting insights for the general business reader and for professionals in the worlds of media, marketing, and advertising.

These innovative books, written by leaders in the business, address the challenges and opportunities of these industries. Some of our authors head their own companies, others have worked their way up to the top of their field in large multinationals. They all share a knowledge of their craft and a desire to enlighten others. We hope readers will find these books as helpful and inspiring as *Adweek*, *Brandweek*, and *Mediaweek* magazines.

CASTING FOR BIG IDEAS

A NEW MANIFESTO FOR AGENCY MANAGERS

ANDREW JAFFE

AN ADWEEK BOOK

WILEY

John Wiley & Sons, Inc.

Published by John Wiley & Sons, Inc., Hoboken, New Jersey.
Published simultaneously in Canada.

Illustrations © copyright by Bob White, Whitefish Studios.

For general information on our other products and services please contact our Customer Care Department within the U.S. at (800) 762-2974, outside the United States at (317) 572-3993 or fax (317) 572-4002.

Wiley also publishes its books in a variety of electronic formats. Some content that appears in print may not be available in electronic books. For more information about Wiley products, visit our web site at www.Wiley.com.

ISBN 0-471-30954-0

Printed in the United States of America

10 9 8 7 6 5 4 3 2 1

CONTENTS

FOREWORD

I loathe fishing. Some of my earliest memories involve me sitting under a tarpaulin, in the rain, watching my dad standing up to his waist in a freezing river, wearing a silly hat. I have no recollection of fish whatsoever—only that my father took his art seriously.

It was with trepidation that I picked up Andrew Jaffe's book. Mercifully, however, the connection between fishing and the ad business is endearingly subtle and deftly woven in. (If you bought this in search of piscatorial tips, you will enjoy the pictures, which enhance the metaphor.)

As a farsighted and occasionally terrifying glimpse into our future, this book is even harder to beat.

It's always a pleasure to read the opinions of someone who agrees with you, or perhaps with whom you agree. Andrew's belief that the advertising business desperately needs a big rethink coincides entirely with my own. For years, agencies have waffled on about "orchestration," and, lately, "360-degree marketing" (the art of going round in circles without ever reaching a conclusion), but have missed the real point. In the first place, they've talked a good game, but have rarely delivered, and in the second, both these buzzwords are media-centric and are about external conditions. The real future will be about *ideas*. Horrifyingly for agencies, the creative product is not only going to be more important, but may well be the *only* product they can sell.

For over a decade it has seemed to me that buying a space and then trying to think of an idea to fill that space is plain daft: Surely the idea must be more powerful than the medium and must therefore come first.

Of course, this was a symptom of the commission system. And even though that mad, unprofessional, and arguably corrupt practice has gone the way of the flat-earth theory, ad agencies persist in issuing maps that contain dire warnings about falling off the edge. Naturally, the arrival of each new medium is greeted by a general bout of

flapping and squawking that the sky is falling, but since chickens can
be hypnotized with a piece of chalk, we can ignore them. Radio didn't
kill print; TV didn't kill radio; the Net won't kill TV; SMS won't kill
the phone. But if you follow the thread, you'll notice that, with every
new means of communication, advertising in its broadest sense had to
become more interesting, more focused, and more relevant. More lik-
able, in fact. More charming.

It seems to me that this is A Good Thing.

While I was spending endless summers watching my father flailing
about (catching mainly trees, I seem to recall, and once or twice, deliri-
ously for spectators, his silly hat), I met two other river-bankers. Both
were poachers. Both nice guys. Each hated the other. Both were neutral
about my old man, as being an irrelevance to the catching of fish.

One was a dynamiter. In a way, very efficient. He got a lot of fish,
but he wasted far more than he caught. And it was an expensive
method. Plus, I bet it *really* annoyed the trout.

The other was a tickler. He lay on a blanket, by a still pool, and
waited for a really fat feller to drop by for a little rest. Then he stroked
its tummy till it went all woozy and smiley, and eased it out. He had
to know exactly where to lie. He had to know exactly how to stroke
the trout, and to do so without its really noticing that it was being
stroked. But he needed no expensive equipment and indulged in no
unseemly thrashing about with a string on a stick. And he got precisely the fish he wanted.

He used charm, you see.

Perhaps we can learn from fishing, after all.

Neil French
Worldwide Creative Director,
Ogilvy & Mather, Singapore

Introduction: The Call for a New Smarter Agency Architecture

If we can discipline ourselves to cast a line with perfection, perhaps we can impose order on—or perceive some inherent order within—the chaos of daily existence.
Howell Raines
Fly Fishing through the Midlife Crisis[1]

This book started out as a primer on agency management. But the more I studied the problems of modern agencies, the more concerned I became about their survival. As if to highlight this fact, last fall, while I was in the midst of finishing this book, Maurice Levy of Publicis Groupe purchased Bcom3, a holding company responsible for the fortunes of two great agency brands—Leo Burnett and D'Arcy (aka D'Arcy Masius Benton & Bowles). A few months later, Levy announced he was shuttering D'Arcy and moving what he could of its $10 billion in global billings and 6,000 employees in 72 countries over to his other holdings—Leo Burnett, Saatchi & Saatchi, and Publicis Advertising.

It was a stunning reminder of how fragile the current leading agencies of the industry really are. Leo Burnett and Saatchi & Saatchi had been in trouble in the mid-1990s but managed to reorganize their businesses and show some profit. D'Arcy had been struggling to rebuild its business for two decades.

Apparently, Levy had concluded that the most elegant solution for his company—at a time when agency owners are looking for economies to sustain earnings—was to do what he could to strengthen three of his networks and let the fourth succumb.

D'Arcy, founded in 1906 in St. Louis and later merged with McManus Inc. and then Benton & Bowles, remains one of the great agency brands of the past century. In distant places like Russia, Brazil, and China, D'Arcy was revered as a leader. To erase such a brand entirely will not only mean the loss of jobs for hundreds and ultimately thousands of employees, it serves as just another weary milestone in the attempts of the industry to restructure.

What can managers of agencies large and small do to survive? To answer this question, the industry must begin an exhaustive reexamination of the agency's basic purpose and abilities. If you are eking out a profit in the current down market, it's easier to assume that you are doing all you can to improve your company's fortunes on your little piece of the river and that it will only take a modest change in the current to start taking fish again.

That would be a correct analysis if there weren't so many external factors well beyond any one agency manager's control eating away at the basic health of the industry. Many clients have taken a fresh look at how their marketing dollars are being spent, concluding, for good or ill, that too much of their advertising budget is wasted. They are pressing for more effective communications at a time when the consumer is putting up new defenses against advertising messages, if not tuning them out altogether. In this climate, it would help if one could reengineer and rethink the agency model to rig it for tomorrow's market instead of hoping that fate and luck will make everything come right.

As Howell Raines says at the beginning of this chapter, it's time to make order out of chaos. To clarify answers and develop new approaches to these ongoing issues, I use parallels to another difficult endeavor: fly-fishing. To excel as an agency manager in today's advertising and marketing services industries, you need several basic skills: patience; the ability to pitch successfully for new business; knowledge of the consumer and the competitive environment; a deep understanding of a wide spectrum of media; an instinctive love of the hunt; and the backing of a great team. With a few notable exceptions, all of these skills have their counterparts in fly-fishing.

In addition, fishing is really a form of hunting. You are stalking a prey and then unleashing your rod and the lure to try to hook the fish. In this metaphor, when going after a new account, the client becomes the prey. It's a question of mastering all your skills to make your agency appealing to the client. Then, having won the client's trust, your prey becomes the consumer whose attention and belief you seek on behalf of the client.

Both of these efforts require a great idea—the right fly tied just the right way given the season, the geography, the lay of the river, and the kind of insects hatching at that time of year—to stir the consumer's interest. You match the hatch in choosing the appropriate lure; you cast just so; you don't worry the line, but leave the fly on or just under the water until the fish bites. Then it's a matter of you and the client using all your skills to make the catch—either a sale or a lasting brand impression that will create revenue downstream.

This, then, is a book about tying great flies—hatching and presenting big ideas that will transform brands and drive a brand message home to the right audience at the right time in just the right way. Lord Leverhulme is credited with the aphorism, "Half of my advertising is wasted—I just don't know which half." The amount of wasted effort might be much greater, but clients have no choice. They have to win over consumers to sample their products or their companies will perish. They have to fish all the time. They are aware that the business of advertising is a high art, and there are few master guides whose every cast is such a masterpiece of precision and art that it is guaranteed to snare fish in large numbers. They're not about to give up on advertising altogether and will tolerate some miscasts in the hope of filling their creels with more consumer dollars over time.

The problem is that in the past few decades the business of devising successful marketing communications has become incredibly harder. Media has proliferated. Brand loyalty has eroded. Distinctions between brands have been harder to define. Moreover, the marketplace is now so saturated with brand messages that consumers have become more adept at recognizing an ad when it hits the water, and have developed increasingly sophisticated filters to keep any marketing messages from wasting space in their brains.

IS IT TIME TO RERIG YOUR GEAR?

This is a crucial time for the industry. It has been consolidating and contracting now for almost 20 years. In the past two decades, your home television has exploded into more than 100 channels; newspapers have lost some of their grip on local audiences; the Internet has come along, giving customers direct access to information about brands; and clients have developed a whole new, nonadvertising kit bag for building brands and talking to consumers.

Yet the typical agency structure and business model has changed almost not at all. The only difference is that its financial managers have had to learn how to charge clients for time-based services rather than live off more generous media commissions. Moreover, new technologies today—at least on television and on the Web—are giving consumers an opportunity to ignore advertising altogether. Effectiveness could deteriorate even further.

While clients are still eager to employ people with vision and the ability to turn around sick brands and make their healthy brands into category leaders, they are more skeptical than ever about the effectiveness of advertising. Indeed, one of the singular failures of the industry has been its inability to come up with any dependable measure to prove the ROI of great, impactful advertising.[2]

In my years as editor of *Adweek* and in the six years I have spent running the Clio Awards, I've been fortunate to visit many of the great agencies of our time—not only in the United States but also around the world. I've become friends with agency managers, creative directors, account planners, strategic planners, media buyers and sellers, and innovative thinkers and marketers. In this book I reflect on their thinking to provide inspiration for others looking for ways to effect meaningful change.

In Part 1 of this book, I take a hard look at traditional roles and departments in the agency and propose a new architecture, reflecting the wisdom of friends and colleagues at many of today's great agencies. I also detail the benefits of such an architecture and how it bolsters your chances when pitching for new business.

In Part 2, I draw upon their wisdom with suggestions for preparing your agency for the future—everything from looking at the way partnerships are offered to recruit top talent to examining whether an agency should venture into new territory like strategic planning, or even take the ultimate leap and sell out to a global ad network.

At the end of each chapter, I offer "Leadership Lessons"—action items suggested by the points made in the chapter. At the end of the book, I've included appendixes that present invaluable lessons from advertising icons Martin Sorrell and MT Rainey, as well as a profile of IDEO, the California firm that produces startling new product designs on a regular basis.

Overall, I hope this book offers the following benefits:

- Rally agencies behind the premise that their highest mission is to empower brands with ideas.
- Determine the resources needed to provide better service to clients and to assure a better return on the client's marketing investment.
- Outline ways that agency architecture needs to change to make it more idea-focused.
- Review the value of certain functions inside agencies in order to upgrade or replace them with more contemporary skill sets.
- Highlight the need for new measuring tools to prove the efficacy of each communications medium and the messages within it.
- Reexamine the potential of the Internet to help speed up processes and connect with consumers.
- Make the modern agency profitable as a business.

Most of all, the agency's central purpose needs to be reconsidered. This isn't a matter of just stripping old rigs of tired fishing lines and replacing them with new ones. This is a time when new skills and new techniques are required to focus on a much bigger prey—the total transformation of a brand by the application of a great marketing idea.

An underlying theme everywhere in this book is the strongly held belief that agencies must embrace a truly media-neutral approach. This is a force being driven by clients who have grown skeptical of the claims about what ads can accomplish in measured media. It also makes sense that a great marketing idea, to have impact, must be crafted with sensitivity to the way it is communicated to the target and explore all the channels available to it.

Agencies must open themselves to a much broader understanding of how best to attack marketing problems. Are agencies expected to revert to their original purpose of brokering media, or do they have a bigger mission with the potential for driving huge increases in sales? Can agencies survive on the business of just making ads, or is their business defending and building brands regardless of channel? What does it matter if the client's purposes are served through an event instead of a TV campaign—especially if the event is more relevant to the target?

The larger the lure, the bigger the fish. This book is meant to help those who are seeking a methodology to transform their companies into an idea-based network. Adopting a new idea focus will seem daunting at first. Just about every function must be overhauled if agencies are to be treasured as something more than mere pipelines for ideas—produced by other, more innovative kinds of companies. It isn't that clients don't need what agencies have traditionally provided in the way of marketing communications. It's that clients are no longer confident agencies truly understand their brands. Or that the ideas they serve up are the best way to communicate a brand.

To compound the present situation, agencies are already being hammered by strategic consultants who get to go upstream of the brand development process to devise effective marketing strategies. A new generation of marketing research companies are entering the fray, capable of not only reading changes in the consumer, but of coming up with ideas for new products and advertising strategies. From the other end, production companies are now working backward, not only making television commercials, but creating ideation units to come up with new ways of pushing a brand into the culture—totally separate from ads and advertising.

WHO WILL PREVAIL ON THIS TRICKIEST OF RIVERS?

The future will no doubt belong to the small and the nimble who can adapt to this evolving new environment. These are agencies led by experienced leaders, who trained in the bigger agencies and then left them out of frustration for what they saw were antiquated systems. These people—just like the leaders of the major agencies who are trying to make them more responsive to change—are the inspiration for this book and its primary voice. Systems don't create and lead agencies, people do. The industry has been blessed with more than 50 years of charismatic leaders. The potential for leadership and vision in even the smallest agency is tremendous.

When I became a subeditor of *Adweek* in the mid-1980s, Joel Babbitt and Joey Reiman, two effervescent 30-somethings, were the toast of the advertising industry in the South, just as Fallon was in the Midwest and Chiat/Day in the West. In 1988, Babbitt and Reiman's $50 million Atlanta agency was bought for the then princely sum of $7 million and joined loosely with two other, larger mid-America shops, GSD&M in Texas and Martin/Williams in Minnesota to give its British owner, Michael Greenlees of Gold Greenlees Trott, dreams of becoming a global player.

After the earn-out, the partners drifted off. Reiman focused more on consulting and teaching. Babbitt moved briefly to New York and then helped establish Channel One, the innovative commercial television news channel for the classroom. After Channel One was sold, Babbitt migrated back to Atlanta to start a second agency, called 360. In 2002, 360 joined with Grey to win the giant BellSouth account, and suddenly Babbitt's agency became the Southern outpost of a great multinational agency network.

It's this continuing birth, death, and rebirth of the industry's progeny that makes advertising so exciting. People with ideas cannot be denied the right to build brands. However, it's very difficult to define the perfect agency manager. One might be an actor (Mary Wells), a classified ad salesman (Bob Schmidt), a comedienne (Linda Kaplan Thayer), a master chef (David Ogilvy), or even a Caribbean charter boat captain (Jim Mullen). Whatever their heritage, they have a passion for the work and enough ambition to see beyond today's disappointments and gird for the future.

What makes for success in one agency and failure in another? Why did Wells Rich Greene succeed wildly in the 1970s and early 1980s and then, after its principal founder retired, self-destruct in the late 1980s? Why did Chiat/Day become everyone's "Agency of the Decade" in the 1980s and then in the next decade nearly collapse—only to be rescued from the scrap heap by a great but once flawed global network, TBWA?

Why have some leading American midsized agencies (Fallon and later Goodby, Silverstein & Partners and Wieden + Kennedy) continued strong through three decades of existence, while other great shops of roughly the same vintage (Levine, Huntley, Schmidt & Beaver; Ammirati & Puris; Ally Gargano; Grace & Rothschild; Angotti Thomas Hedge) flamed out and died? How does one explain the explosive growth of Deutsch, a once sleepy New York agency whose control in 1992 was passed from father to son—and in 2000 was sold to IPG for $267 million? At the same time, one of the oldest names in American advertising, N.W. Ayer, the agency that created such famous brand lines as "I'd walk a mile for a Camel," "A diamond is forever," and "Reach out and touch someone," had its name retired and its accounts quietly passed to a new, fast-growing New York agency, The Kaplan Thaler Group.

The answer is that while the agency world takes a very conservative approach to its own systemic problems—and seldom even discusses them openly with clients, employees, or the public—the massive forces of the marketplace are decreeing change. The growth of Deutsch in New York and Los Angeles and now Crispin Porter Bogusky in Miami and Los Angeles is due in large part to the contrarian views of leaders who aren't afraid to experiment and come up with radical new approaches to client problems.

These new lights are determined not to be brought down by the arteriosclerosis that destroyed the other great houses of Madison Avenue in the past half century: Dancer Fitzgerald Sample, Wells Rich Greene, Compton, Lintas, Jordan Case McGrath, Bozell Jacobs

Kenyon & Eckhardt, Benton & Bowles, Harper Needham Stears, Doyle Dane Bernbach, Chiat/Day, and now Ayer and D'Arcy.

TIME FOR A NEW CHANNEL FOCUS

If I'm right that the traditional media focus of agencies no longer serves the needs of clients, then there's no doubt that great changes are about to take place. The only question becomes one of defining change—and coming up with new ways of meeting old goals without tossing the vintage bamboo rods of advertising into the garage.

This book is meant to challenge anyone who supports the status quo. The ideas described herein, except where expressly attributed to someone in quotes, are mine alone and will hopefully intrigue and perhaps enlighten. They might be wrong—but something has to done. The current dysfunctional model can't be sustained. The increasing barriers to profitability demand new approaches.

Becoming media-neutral is essential for agency success, as I discuss in Part 1. It's no doubt going to be a difficult passage, as clients have grown accustomed to getting many services in a package once funded by generous 15 percent commissions. Clients have little or no patience with agency screams of pain and indecision. Agencies strong in creative or some other focus will be able to charge a premium for their services, but that may not carry the day. Agencies with the broadest palette and the more innovative approach to communication will more likely prevail, or clients will further unbundle their spending and hire best-of-class specialists for each aspect of the marketing communications process—leaving agencies the more mundane role of becoming conduits, not creators.

A few years ago, in the early 1990s, I visited the head of a multinational network to talk about the impact of the Internet. The executive had a computer on his desk—but he needed help from an assistant to access the Internet. When we started to talk about the intricacies of digital marketing, he had to call for the vice president specializing in that area to field my questions. He was charged with leading his agency into the future, but our talk was often interrupted by calls from the head of the parent company, who was more interested in cutting costs than building new revenue streams. Neither my host nor his boss had much interest in new media because they thought it offered scant help in finding solutions to their problems. They were ready to acknowledge that the Internet was the medium of the future, but they were hoping to retire before its power was manifest.

In 2000 and 2001, the Internet advertising model collapsed and these executives no doubt breathed a sigh of relief. Those whose fortunes depended on television and print felt vindicated. Meanwhile, Internet usage has continued to climb. Now we are beginning to see broadband introduced into homes and offices, giving content creators the option of sending full-motion video at 30 frames a second, with no download delay, not over the TV or movie screen—but through the computer. The future didn't go away—it's just that the capital markets funding its infrastructure needed to cool off for a while and devise a more realistic, profit-driven, return-on-investment model.

Today we have the opportunity to project dynamic brand messages in TV-like commercials over the computer—with the added dimension of enabling the viewer to interact with the originator of such messages. Coming the other way is the impatience of consumers who tell interviewers they no longer want to watch ads because they find them a nuisance and an unreliable source of information, along with a demand that content over the Internet be free (even commercial-free), leaving everyone wondering who's going to pay for content in the future.

Eventually a new model has to evolve. The Internet won't be forever free, because premium content costs money to create. But that doesn't mean that commercials and static print ads need to be replicated in their present form. Changes are afoot to enable the consumer to *choose whichever ads he or she wants to watch* and to offer a more transparent barter of content in exchange for advertising, much as occurs today in magazines, newspapers, and broadcast television.

The model of the ad agency must change, too, in response to the opportunities provided by new media and new demands from clients and consumers for messages to be more relevant and timely. These issues are outlined in more detail in Chapter 5.

IS THERE A PENALTY FOR HOLDING BACK?

"If agencies don't change, what will happen?" says DDB chairman Keith Reinhard. "Well, when everything becomes content, which it will, the next generation of TiVo will make it as easy to use as your cell phone, as it will edit out our work. So people will just ignore our commercials.

"Once you have the brand foundation in place, then what's going to be needed is a Leonard Bernstein who understands all the instruments and knows when to bring in the tympani, when to bring in direct marketing, when the bassoon plays, and when public relations plays. And that's the role we don't have yet."

Using the metaphor of fly-fishing as our guide, with its emphasis on graceful execution and precision casting, let's see if we cannot divine a more sensible agency management model for the future.

PART 1

Agency Architecture

CHAPTER 1

Agency Architecture: Getting It Right from the Beginning

There is a form of fly fishing that is like a spent spinner, fading and dying. . . . The venerable winged wet fly, once popular and a staple in a trout fisher's fly book, has lost favor.

Roger Menard
My Side of the River[1]

This book is about the ingredients that go into the making of a successful agency. There are certain givens. The first is the bedrock tenet of modern marketing: Differentiate your brand. Agencies must learn early on to develop unique cultures and capabilities that separate them from the competition. Otherwise, they risk being marginalized by clients.

Even the label *full service* is suspect in today's marketplace. No young agency can afford to offer all the above-the-line and below-the-line specialties such a phrase suggests, and, if it did, would that agency be any different from more established agencies making the same claim?

How do you go about making your agency unique and competitive? You might start by looking at your agency's architecture.

The internal structure of most agencies is like Roger Menard's "spent spinner." It is built on a rigid, silo-like departmental model that goes back more than 50 years. This was the time of the Organization Man, when agencies and their clients were built like the Pentagon—with everything neatly in its place. Since then, the structures of clients have been updated and streamlined—but agencies never were.

Under the silo model, everyone has a function and reports to a silo leader. If you're a media buyer, you sit in the media department. If you're a creative person, you get to sit, work, and play in the creative department. Occasionally you see people from other silos in meeting rooms, in the cafeteria, or on company picnics. The only time you physically work as a team is in a new business pitch, where for a time everyone gets to eat from the same pizza carton, spending hours rehearsing and polishing the pitch.

Does this really make sense? Shouldn't agencies be discipline-neutral, freewheeling structures that form and re-form for a specific purpose, without regard to titles, departments, and seniority? Shouldn't they exhibit an open architecture, in design, purpose, and business model, that is inclusive and makes everyone feel equally part of the creative process?

To be idea-neutral, you need a brief and very little else. But in advertising, everyone brings a preconceived notion of what is required. The pressure is on to make ads, not necessarily to achieve quantifiable results. Results growing out of advertising are very ephemeral things, because in actual fact you cannot measure, except in rare instances, the precise impact of a communication on consumer behavior. Sure, the famous Aaron Burr commercial in the "Got milk?" campaign made people think of how nice it would be to drink a glass milk after eating a peanut butter sandwich. But did the ad drive milk sales? Well, it's hard to tell. If you ask consumers why they buy a product, they don't usually answer, "Because I saw a great ad last night on television." They say something like, "Because I need it and I trust this brand."

Eventually, your gut will tell you what works. Great advertising is memorable and strikes an emotional chord with the target. That should translate into sales results or brand awareness. How do you get great advertising? Well, not by assembling your ad team and saying, "Guys, we've got to come up with a great TV campaign." Whoa! Slow down. What you need first is an idea.

Really good ideas usually spring from very open thinking. Don't start by defining the media channel or the celebrity you want in an ad or the music to go behind it. Start with the idea.

That may be harder than you think. Especially in this new environment where clients are looking for ways to communicate an idea beyond traditional media. For agencies to support a media-neutral approach, there is a critical need for a new architecture—one that breaks down the silo model. First, cultures of mature agencies need to be overhauled to reignite the attitudes and work ethics of their people. Furthermore, every five years or so, the agency partners should assemble and reconsider their current model, asking themselves the consultant's standard question, "If you were starting this company tomorrow, how would you design it?"

If the answer isn't, "Make an exact replica of what we are today," then you have your work cut out for you.

The first issue in redefining culture is to agree on your mission. What do you want your agency to do? The obvious next question: How should we organize to best perform that mission? Everything in advertising seems to resist change. Ossification of culture begins to take place in months, sometimes weeks after an agency is born. Perhaps such an early definition is a natural development that allows people to define their roles and get on to the more serious business of client service and idea creation. But advertising is an ever-changing endeavor. Agencies have to reform every few years to ensure their relevance and ability to deliver a superior product.

This is not a new thought. As the great manufacturing companies started to experience the recession and market dislocations of the late 1980s and early 1990s, the call went out for something called *process reengineering*. Reengineering was meant to refer to the study of the processes and organization structures that go into the making of an efficient factory or business. But in the 1989–1990 recession, the phrase came to stand for laying off large numbers of people and downsizing.

In fact, process reengineering, when done right, is a tremendously energizing exercise. Interestingly, there were conferences on the subject throughout the advertising industry, but few agencies ever seriously tried it.

One that did is Pittsburgh-based MARC Advertising, which dared to knock down walls and endure a traumatic, formal reengineering process. MARC USA CEO Tony Bucci recalls the epiphany he had while attending an American Association of Advertising Agencies annual meeting in 1992: "We had been growing, but the problem was that as we added revenues, we added costs, too. People were working nights and weekends. I didn't see how they could work any harder. But we couldn't improve our margins. I knew there was something inherently wrong. I knew I needed to do something dramatically different, but didn't know what it was."

At the annual meeting, he slipped into a workshop on process reengineering led by a consultant from Arthur Andersen. "He told how he had gone into the media department of an agency and slashed what he saw as a duplication of activities. I thought, 'Holy cow, this might be just what we need.' "

Bucci got paired with the speaker on the golf course and eventually decided to hire Arthur Andersen and to turn MARC (which in 1993 was billing about $64 million) on its ear. The Andersen team spent six months studying the agency's problems and then began changing people's tasks, reforming departments, and cutting down the number of steps it took to make ads and to service clients. The result was not only that profitability soared, but also that people felt energized. Within a few months of the completion of its new structure, the agency started to add new clients and billings. In 1994 it jumped to $79 million and the following year almost doubled to $154 million. Then it began acquiring agencies in other cities—two years later it was billing $300 million.

The reengineering process of the silo model that existed at MARC has never really stopped, Bucci notes, because the agency now is constantly reexamining itself as it grows—especially as it adds new offices. As Bucci says, "Too many people get into process reengineering and think they're finished. But you have to change the mentality of people—most importantly of senior management. You have to move from process to mind-set—and not just of staff but of their leaders."

The MARC system of reorganization is based on a multistep process involving planning, discussion, and training by every constituency—even clients. Every move is preceded by weeks and months of discussion about employees' roles and functions. Bucci is very logical. He likes to work according to a plan—one that is understood and supported by senior staff. He spends a lot of time in meetings and retreats, discussing various approaches and trying to gain consensus from his associates on ways to attack problems. When there is agreement, though, the agency is not afraid to tear down walls and processes and introduce new approaches and architecture.

Bucci feels he's now about halfway to his goal. "I laid out what I call a *vision horizon*—an outline of where we wanted to be in 10 years. We've done it in three-year increments. We're growing, but we're still in the formulation of our first stage," he says. A decade later the agency has grown tenfold and is billing about $650 million, with offices in Pittsburgh, Chicago, Indianapolis, Miami, and Dallas. As such, it stands, with The Richards Group and Wieden + Kennedy, as one of the top five independently owned agencies in the United States.

Bucci is tough on himself and the industry. "We're not anything yet," he said in an interview in late 2002, "because we're still re-creating as we acquire and constantly adjusting what are to be our strengths and what will be our product niche. Come back and look at us in a couple of years—by then I would bet that we'll be on the West Coast and probably in Boston and billing above $1 billion."

As for his friends in the AAAA, Bucci says, "The biggest problem for this industry is that it's not training its young people to be leaders. Everyone is so focused on technical magic. What we need are business leaders who can help clients find the answers to their problems."

IMMERSING YOUR TEAM IN THE WORK

Some agencies, following the lead of Messner Vetere Berger McNamee Schmetterer Euro RSCG in New York, have created "war rooms" for clients. In this mode, the teams put all the work relating to the client and the competition on moving or layered walls. The team is thus surrounded with "windows" of data in much the same way a computer desktop can be made to represent all the ideas critical to the strategic evolution of the brand.

But such war rooms are a temporary affair. Few agencies can afford permanently to allocate communal space to a single client. After the meeting ends, the team disperses and all the materials are packed into a cabinet. It is a momentary thing.

In trying to create a company devoted solely to the creation of ideas, some agencies might decide to take the war room's communal space to a new level. They might surround everyone with ideas, good and bad, and keep them working in close proximity to one another.

These agencies might ask: Isn't there a more productive structure that would better define people by mission rather than discipline? Function follows form in a service business. Just because everyone knows where to sit when they come into work doesn't mean they are organized properly to fight the battles of a modern idea agency. In fact, with the advent of computers, most people spend the day focused on the screen in front of them and physical architecture has become less important.

Consider what it would mean to organize the creative department to include media planners, account planners, art directors, and copy-writers. Another department might be called "production" and include traffic people, media buyers, and junior account people, all focused on keeping the work on budget and on schedule—the *action* part of the agency rather than the *thinking* part.

Strategic planning, senior account management, and research could be isolated into a third grouping. Even better, this group could operate under a separate brand name and be sited on another floor or in a different building—so that clients meeting this group would get the impression they were in the presence of strategists whose work was not included in the advertising budget.

Imagine the effect this would have on everyone. Certainly account people might complain that they had been excluded from the creative process, but at least they would be asking to be part of that process rather than to control it. Creatives would gain a broader focus.

Strategic planning would be recognized as a premium service. Traffic people might teach account people their negotiating skills— and learn from their new teammates more about the client business they were servicing. Media buyers might just enjoy the hustle and bustle of the traffic department. As Tony Bucci can tell you, even moving around the desks and retitling people has a dramatic, energiz-ing effect on an agency's culture. The point of the exercise is that this kind of reengineering serves to redefine an agency's mission and reex-amine its functionality.

DEPARTMENTS VERSUS BRAND TEAMS

For a time, many leading creative agencies in the late 1980s and early 1990s—Chiat/Day and Carmichael Lynch, to name a few—played with the idea of reorganizing themselves into brand units rather than on the traditional department model. Instead of separating accounting and creative functions, people were seated together in account teams. Agencies contracted with architects to redesign their interiors and bring in movable furniture and walls so that account people, planners, creatives, and others devoted to a single account could be grouped together on a single floor or within a walled area.

Jack Supple, creative director of Carmichael Lynch, recalls with some horror an experiment with what he calls "the group system." He says, "We would form into groups where they actually had their own P&L built around the accounts they managed. In those days, account people really had the numbers of the creatives—we were pretty much captive, right under the thumb of the account people who ran the accounts."

Supple continues, "I remember once I was sitting in the office of a creative, kicking around an idea, when from the next office someone said: 'No, you can't do that.' The account guy was sitting right next door. He didn't understand that creatives need to have an opportunity to be stupid and think things you can't do. We like to put them on the wall and consider them and then take them down. But he was already telling us what we couldn't think about."

"When we moved offices a few years later to our present building, I insisted creative people sit in proximity so that they can bounce ideas off each other. Because a lot of our creative power comes from just casually checking things out. And one creative person sees something hot going on nearby and starts getting new ideas about his own problem. It's infectious."

Today there's a realization that really good thinking has little to do with how the desks are sited, but there's still a question about whether the old architecture is interfering with clear brand thinking. Many agency leaders think it is—but they're still not sure what to do about it. In the rest of this chapter I'll explore the fundamental roles within the agency, asking how they can be molded for a new agency model.

RETHINKING ACCOUNT SERVICE

No department is more deserving of a major rethink than account service. Clients, in increasing numbers, are turning to professional marketing consultants for help with their brands. Agencies are being forced to execute strategies created by others. Meanwhile, in the rush of the past decade to bring down costs, the account service function has been pushed down to more junior and less-well-trained personnel, who are asked to spend more time on process and less on strategic thinking. Because of this and other factors, it has become difficult for agencies to attract graduates from the nation's top business schools—partly because the opportunity for developing a brand is stronger on the client side and partly because the pay is better at brands.

"We're hoping the pendulum is starting to change back in the agency's favor," says Michael Donahue, executive vice president of the American Association of Advertising Agencies. "Graduates in their late 20s and early 30s don't have the kind of choices they used to have with Wall Street and Big Six accounting firms. There's a diminishing market in the consulting and money industries for people with a more humanistic, right brain approach to life."

Donahue predicts that young people more interested in the intuitive way advertising agencies work will still be attracted to the business—even though Wall Street houses and consultancies sometimes offer higher starting salaries.

"In some ways this competition between McKinsey and agencies has been overblown," he says. "McKinsey says it's in the engagement business. Well, agencies are in the relationship business—with clients and with the marketplace. If you're in the engagement business, you can ride in and ride out. Agencies have accountability. They have to stick around to see if the solutions they recommend actually work."

But just because agencies are again able to attract the best graduates doesn't mean they know how to use them properly. Telling a Harvard Business School graduate skilled in marketing strategy to ensure that advertising for a soap account (made by others at the agency) is on time and on budget isn't necessarily the same challenge as launching a dot-com business or finding the venture capital to turn around a steel plant.

Agencies need to either recommit to account service or fold its function into other parts of the agency. Just having junior people trafficking ads and budgets and dressing them up with big titles is not the answer.

SAVING ACCOUNT SERVICE BY KILLING IT

A lot has been said over the past decade about the gradual downgrading of account service. One agency, Roche Macaulay & Partners in Toronto, dared to create a new model—without any account executives. At RM&P, each client is assigned to a senior traffic chief, who used to be called a *project manager* and more recently was retitled *business manager* (BM). The agency, which bills about $50 million with clients like Mercedes-Benz, Coca-Cola (Nestea), and Reebok, currently has four such business managers who keep the work on budget and on time. Clients have learned to interact on a regular basis with the business manager—just as they did with an account executive in the past. At various times during the year, a *strategic planner* (SP), who has an intimate knowledge of the client's business and the category, studies the effectiveness of the work and addresses strategic opportunities for the brand.

It may be hard for many believe that there is no one person responsible for the account on a day-to-day basis. But Roche insists his clients have learned to appreciate the system. Tara Ruoso, for instance, has worked nine years as a product/business manager at RM&P. Her accounts include Johnson & Johnson, Nestlé, Coca-Cola (Nestea), and RCA. She doesn't see herself as a glorified traffic person, but admits the dreariest part of the job is "all the administrative paperwork."

Contrast her with Trent Fulton, who has worked at RM&P as a strategic planner for two years. Like Ruoso, he came out of account management. His accounts include Purina dog food, Mackenzie Financial, and Coca-Cola (Nestea). He considers the most interesting part of his job working with senior management on the client side, and he has the luxury of having time to drill down to find the unique selling proposition (USP) of a brand.

"Our thinking," says Geoffrey Roche, founder of RM&P and a creative director by training, "was that the role of account person had been made less effective by virtue of the fact that account people were being asked to wear too many hats: trafficking, account service, strategic planning, and profit and loss control. So we split the functions into two, allowing the project manager to run the day-to-day machinations and the planner to concentrate on the strategic side of the account, not only day-to-day but a year or two out."

Roche says that promoting highly motivated traffic people to work directly with clients is fairly straightforward. Traffic people have been marginalized and underused, he says. Because they are so good at working internally with deadlines and externally with postproduction facilities, it's thought they cannot do anything else. Training them to take on more responsibility and assume a higher profile was fairly easy. But finding the right kind of person for strategic planning was more difficult.

"Traditional account executives were not necessarily the most strategically minded individuals," Roche says. "They could come up with a strategy, but it was a paragraph in a brief, not a single, distinct positioning for client. They tended to be more client-centric instead of consumer-centric. And account planners were just the opposite. They were used to working with creative people and liked to concentrate only on consumers. The two disciplines have to meet. You have to be able to talk to clients about pricing and distribution—and then turn around and look at how the advertising works and what is going on with consumers."

The agency has maintained its unique approach since it opened in 1991 and today has some imitators in the Toronto market. Former RM&P partner Andy Macaulay started his own agency, Zig, which features a similar structure. Labatt's beer, with its giant $70 million account, has helped start an agency, Grip, led by four former Roche employees, and calls its account people "planners" and has upgraded the traffic people to work as project and business managers.

Few agencies, though, seem in a hurry to reexamine the account management function. Some are afraid of asking clients to relate to two handlers. Roche admits that some clients are uncomfortable with RM&P's bifurcated system. "We usually can sense this in the pitch," he says. "If they keep asking us how it works and who is going to be responsible for the business, then we know we are going to have a problem."

JUST CALLING SOMEONE STRATEGIC PLANNER
MAY NOT BE ENOUGH

The question remains: How can agencies hire and deploy better-trained strategists as account managers and then, in the new fee-based-environment, charge adequately for their services and keep them from getting lost in the "process" part of agency life?

Perhaps admitting that for some in the agency, process and not strategic thinking is their primary job might be a first step to unraveling the mess in which agencies have found themselves. For others, it's really a matter of reconstructing the agency so that people work more effectively and that the look and feel of the agency is directed at producing ideas and not widgets. Agency architecture cries out for experimentation. Hopefully, there will be new models in the future that will answer this question, either from inside the agency world or from the allied worlds of design and even architecture.

"When you think about it, our creative ideas are the one thing we don't get paid for, says DDB's Keith Reinhard. It's the one thing we give away. The mistake was made 100 years ago when the advertising agent's job was to place the client's ad copy in the newspapers. One day, the agent said to the client, 'You know, I could help you a little bit by adding pictures and maybe rewriting your copy.'

"The client said, 'What does that cost?'

"The advertising agent replied, 'Oh, nothing, because we're going to get rich on the commission.' "

Reinhard believes agencies would have to set up wholly new companies through which to channel agency-originated ideas for new products, new brands, and advertising equities in order to be able to charge separately for these services—either through the direct sale of ideas or by charging a licensing fee for their use. He says, "If a traditional agency tried to charge a current client for such ideas, the client would say, 'Get out of here. For 100 years, you've been giving me your best ideas free in exchange for a media commission or a fixed fee.' Our best chance might be to set up a New Co [new company] specializing in the sale and licensing of ideas. At least until marketers get used to the fact that an idea is the most valuable thing we provide."

RETHINKING THE ORGANIZATION AS A WHOLE

A similar downgrading of stature and pay has occurred in media departments. In the 1990s, as clients began questioning media charges and became interested in achieving more clout in their media buys, they turned to giant unbundled media shops that could buy TV or print more efficiently. To do this, clients had to suspend some of their conflict rules—and accept the occasional disconnect that comes from buying and planning media in one place and ordering creative services from another.

Agency heads weren't able to come up with an argument against this kind of unbundling, so gradually the media-buying function withered and some agencies struggled just to maintain some planning expertise. Now, innovative ideas for building brands can come from media sellers, too. It's assumed that magazine publishers and TV and radio ad people are interested only in selling space. But the smart ones try to understand a brand's needs and come up with new ways to stretch budgets and express brand ideas. Without access to these people through day-to-day negotiations, such ideas are never heard.

Meanwhile there is a new and more desperate need for better strategic thinking. Some agencies find themselves lacking the intellectual capital to stay competitive. Given this confusion, it's certainly time for a serious reexamination of what the modern advertising agency should be.

Nick Brien, U.S. president for new business development with Starcom MediaVest and a former agency head himself at Leo Burnett/London, believes agency architecture is about to change. "I would say frankly the whole agency structure which currently is silo functionality in departments needs to be reformed," says Brien. "Departments are increasingly redundant in a fast-changing marketing world. I want to enhance the thinking process of the agency and make it more seamless. If I had, say, the four disciplines of an agency—account management, strategy planning, media, and creative—in one place, I would ask how they could be reworked with one goal in mind: conceptual creativity."

Some agencies are thinking more about people and functions than about architecture. Agencies like Fallon are trying to identify "thought leaders" and empower them to take a commanding lead in driving the work—no matter where they reside in the agency's structure. In fact, at Fallon, management identifies such people and moves them around in the organization in an effort to increase the strength of each department.

"Obviously, in the interview process, we are looking for leaders," says cofounder Fred Senn. "Was [former Fallon creative director] Jamie Barrett marked as a leader from the beginning? Absolutely. We've identified a pool of thought leaders who can provide sound strategic thinking on board-level issues. They become a shadow board, if you will. And there's a difference between your level in the organization as a manager or department head and how we feel about you as a thought leader. Some thought leaders would rather be doers than managers, and that's fine by us."

Fred Senn, Pat Fallon, and the rest of the current Fallon management team spend several hours every few months discussing arcane subjects like the qualities fundamental to a modern agency leader. "We have come up with a dozen different models for thought leadership," says Senn. "We have motivational leadership, inspirational leadership, integrity leadership, value leadership, creative leadership, and on and on. To create organizational capacity you need to perpetually train and grow leaders. As a result, as we've grown as a company, we have come to depend on this group. Go back to early years. Up until we were 60 or 70 or even 100 people, the leadership came from the five founding partners. Today that's impossible."

WHO HAS THE BEST BLUEPRINT?

In the end, agency owners have to make some critical decisions. Even the giant New York shops can't afford to be truly full service anymore.

Increasingly, they are pushing resources into branded subsidiaries and separate profit centers to better track performance and sell each service separately to the client.

Most clients have learned to cherry-pick anyway—going to one agency for advertising, another for media planning, and somewhere else for strategic planning or research. Some, like Coca-Cola, Anheuser-Busch, and McDonald's, have even begun disbursing creative assignments to competing "roster" agencies, so a brand may have an ad aimed at youths produced by one agency and another ad aimed at an older segment produced somewhere else.

The trick is to decide early on which core competencies you are going to offer and not to get sucked into the "everything for everybody" model. "We have remained very faithful to what we originally were," says John Drake, CEO and sole remaining cofounder of Atlanta's Cole Henderson Drake. Drake and his new partners are still pledged to providing "a superior communications product tied to smart marketing strategies." He sees all advertising agencies as having the mission to develop communications that have "the potential to change the client's business." But Drake's agency is willing to work with other companies if the client needs services outside CHD's skill set.

Agency chiefs constantly agonize over which parts of the client's marketing budget might be about to go somewhere else. The urge is to respond to clients demanding more with, "But we have that . . . ," when *seemingly* it would take only one more hire to give an agency expertise in a new area. However, new disciplines mean overhead, training, and experience, and they require integration. Agencies have to decide in which areas they're going to be leaders and in which areas they're going to have to partner with someone else. Chiat/Day experimented with setting up an interactive design unit and drew back when it discovered it couldn't produce work equal to its advertising product. Leo Burnett funneled tens of millions of dollars into broadening its resource base as it struggled to maintain service for its 15 percent commission clients. Then, over the past decade, as clients moved to a fee-based model, it had to shut down or cut back such units.

Bob Schmetterer of Euro RSCG also believes agencies have to be reorganized to get away from the 1990s practice of compartmentalizing each new discipline into a separately branded unit with its own P&L. To do so, he feels, only encourages people to try to sell the client separate solutions. As a result, he's taken all of Euro's dozens of U.S. holdings, including 11 separate advertising agencies, and reorganized them into two giant constellations. One centers on the old Messner agency in New York and the other on the old Tatham Laird in Chicago.

"We think the key to wherever we are today and wherever we want to be tomorrow is to think in a media-neutral way," says Schmetterer. "Our goal is not to make more money but to do the right thing for our clients. We wanted an agency organization that housed all media disciplines—database marketing, direct, interactive, promotion, event marketing, and public relations—in a single agency, with a single P&L.

"One of the problems I have with the phrase 'advertising agency' is that by itself it's self-limiting, when in fact the meaning of advertising is much broader. My view requires reshaping what the ad agency looks like, to ensure it's far more a generalist creative organization than a bunch of specialists in creative advertising. We call this effort Project Power of One. And we believe so strongly in it, we've just rolled it out in France, where we took 25 agencies and created just one, Euro RSCG France."

WHERE'S THE REAL POT OF GOLD?

CHD's John Drake and others—extending as high as WPP CEO Martin Sorrell, who now oversees a vast empire that includes Ogilvy & Mather, Young & Rubicam, J. Walter Thompson, and Wunderman (the leading direct agency)—have bemoaned the fact that agencies have lost out to consultants their role of being "an integral and indispensable part" of the marketing strategy process. That remains the leading conundrum: How can agencies generate and charge for truly big ideas for their clients?

If the answer is to charge 15 percent commissions, well, that train has left the station and is never coming back. "The breakdown of the 15 percent commission is old news," says Ben Wiener, managing partner of the Los Angeles office of *WONGDOODY*. "That system was predicated on clients spending lots of money on media and production. Now clients are pressing us to come up with solutions that don't necessarily call for a print or TV campaign. There's less enthusiasm for a 30-second spot that costs $400,000 to shoot. Agencies are being asked to do a lot more. We need to find ways of delivering more impact for much less money."

A broader discussion of how agencies will face this vital question in the future can be found at the end of this book. But agency architects must recruit to their cause strategic thinkers. Not just people with vision and a gut instinct for what a brand should be, but people who can organize their thoughts and support their premises with the kinds of data and proof offered by professional brand strategists. In the end, if agencies continue to give away their best thinking as part of the advertising package instead of spinning it off into separately branded consulting units with this mission, then their only hope is to develop ways to charge for the time of these superstrategists.

This is a worst-case scenario. Agencies would stand to gain more if they could persuade the client of the value of their ideas and sell the client on new forms of compensation. Agencies must learn how to fight for rights to their intellectual property and fees for ideas that prove to be huge drivers of the brand and that help propel the brand and the advertising idea into unforeseen platforms and media.

All of this calls for a new commitment to making the ideas that an agency generates distinct and apart from the day-to-day communications it produces. If an agency does not or will not pitch and package this deliverable separately, then it has no hope of expecting the client to regard it as worth much. Such a reexamination of the fundamental purpose of the modern agency has tremendous implications for the agency architect. Some agencies have tried to keep different disciplines in-house for fear of losing their sense of integration and equality. Others, like Fallon and, on a much larger scale, DDB, have started by building separate design and corporate image consultancies and then branching out and opening a true strategic marketing consultancy—with different personnel, work space, budgets, and clients.

An agency in the United Kingdom, Rainey Kelly Campbell Roalfe, which now serves as the London office of Young & Rubicam, began with the premise that the agency's primary function was coming up with big ideas. It offered clients a three-phase process. In the first phase, the four founding partners, all distinguished advertising veterans, charged by the hour for studying the client's business and marketing. Research was conducted on the brand, the consumer, and the marketplace. At the end of this period, the agency provided the client with a formal analysis of the brand and its opportunities.

From there, the client was encouraged to go to the second phase, where the partners were asked to come up with a strategic advertising idea based on their research. If the client wished, it could then purchase this idea for a hefty fee and rechart its business based on it—either through other agencies or through Rainey Kelly. Should it choose to work with Rainey Kelly the agency would charge for its work on a flat hourly basis without the usual markup. There were no cost-plus charges for any work—such as production—that the agency jobbed out.

The model is still in use today for all but a handful of clients that the now $400 million agency inherited when it sold itself in 1999 and became the London office of Young & Rubicam. A good example of the agency's idea-based work has been its 10-year-old campaigns for Virgin Atlantic Airways, building the upstart into a formidable competitor of British Airways.

The advantage of Rainey Kelly's approach is that it focuses clients, in a very unique way for this industry, on the fact that *conceptual* creative thinking should be paid at a higher premium than ordinary *executional* creative thinking, because a core conceptual idea can have an explosive effect on a brand's grip on the consumer. This simple but radical approach suddenly transforms an agency from being an agent to being regarded as a creative consultancy. (See Appendix B for further discussion of this subject.)

Many agencies started down this path over the past decade when they added account planning to the mix. However, most agencies that have grown an account planning function have defined it as an adjunct to the creative department rather than as a stand-alone service. As a result, although it has come to replace the old agency research department, it has lost any chance of being viewed by the client as a distinct product for which a separate charge outside the normal advertising budget is justified. Without that final step, account planning will always be a stepchild in the agency's process— and will be priced accordingly.

THE NEED FOR AN ANNUAL BRAND AUDIT
AND REFIT

Even small agencies should try to put in place some kind of proprietary process of field research and analysis that gives clients definitive answers about the marketplace. Every brand could benefit from a full-scale audit once a year. This should never be an amateur, on-the-fly affair; rather, agencies should insist on it being costed as part of the overall marketing budget and refuse to work for clients who won't accept it as integral part of smart marketing. The consumer is never constant. Competing brands are always changing their positions. A ship owner would never go to sea without a compass that has been recalibrated regularly. Similarly, agencies should insist on regular measurement of their communications' effectiveness because an understanding of how they fit into the overall brand universe is central to keeping the brand strategy on course.

Once an agency becomes grounded in the positioning of a client's brands, it can begin to advise the client on issues like media expenditures, new advertising approaches, new markets, and even new products. Whole books have been written on this subject.[2] But the first challenge facing anyone launching or reengineering an agency should be to make sure its thinking processes are strongly based and salable.

Moving from this platform, the agency then has to determine what its deliverables will be and which areas of marketing can be left to other specialty agencies. We may even have reached a point where agencies of record won't be asked to create advertising. This was the case with Coca-Cola when, for a decade, it chose to use a spectrum of agencies for creative advertising ideas while retaining McCann-Erickson as its primary channel for distributing those ad ideas around the world.

The hardest problem for WONGDOODY and other young agencies that don't have a well-defined event marketing or promotions division is to formalize the protocols for the delivery of such services. This isn't a question of coming up with a kiosk at a trade show or a point-of-purchase tent card on a retail display. We're talking about big ideas to push a brand into the culture—such as the steamy catalog that Abercrombie & Fitch published in the mid-1990s to expand dramatically its teenage following.

"I'm not sure anyone has it figured out quite right," says WONGDOODY's Ben Wiener. "What's really clear is that agencies have to offer a lot more than advertising. I like getting clients used to a non-advertising budget. That way agencies may start to be perceived as an intellectual creative resource beyond just fillers of airtime or magazine space."

EVENTUALLY THE IDEA HAS TO BE EXPRESSED IN CONCRETE FORM

Agencies are also doers. They continue to be expected to prepare and deliver specific communications (i.e., advertising campaigns) as the result of work by a broad array of in-house specialists, creatives, TV producers, print departments, media buyers, traffickers, accountants, messengers, and back-office specialists.

Someone has to head this team. For a time, that may continue to be the senior account executive—but a few agencies around the world are experimenting with designating other members as account team leaders. As long as the person can exhibit leadership in pulling together all parts of the day-to-day marketing and can ensure that the work comes in on time and within budget, clients really don't care about job titles.

In addition, at some agencies, media planning is growing in importance. Such agencies are trying to build media buying and planning beyond placement analysis and negotiation into a new strategic arena. This requires a new media-neutral philosophy that puts a higher premium on what creates the greatest brand impression than on billings and media clout. Kirshenbaum Bond & Partners has developed a reputation for doing stunts that create a buzz around a brand—even without advertising—in ways that drive word of mouth or involve the consumer in brand loyalty programs that have the same effect.[3]

If an agency wants to move into the field of corporate communications, it is going to need a strong public relations and collateral division. If it is going to claim expertise in direct marketing, it will (at the very least) need a good research and DM-focused creative department. Other fields attracting attention include corporate design and logos, packaging and product design, interior and environmental design, event marketing and interactive, including Web design and digital customer relationship marketing.

In considering the addition of these competencies, the agency must ask whether it can claim to be "best of class" in all its offerings. Sooner or later, clients are going to balk at being sold services simply because they are offered and owned by the same company that delivers their advertising. If these ancillary services can't compete for non-advertising clients, either improve them or shut them down. They will serve only to degrade the overall quality of the agency and cause the client to seek other providers.

The central issue to designing an effective and profitable agency is to minimize protocols and bureaucracy. In the old model, large agencies had creative review boards and other committees to approve ideas before they were presented to the client. These layers added cost and time to the production of effective communications. In the reengineering wave of the early 1990s, when agency costs were examined closely, many such structures had to be dismantled. No one likes to lay off staff, but layers usually add time and cost to the production of ideas. They are added in times of growth, but it shouldn't take a recession to pare them back.

"Flatter is better," is still the smart rule. In all organizations, there is always a question of span of control by leaders. No one should have more than five or six direct reports. An agency of, say, 100 people shouldn't have more than two layers separating a working employee from a partner. In the end, if clients are dissatisfied, they should be able to talk directly to a partner of the agency who understands their business and can easily address their problems. Meanwhile, agency heads should audit at least biannually how many steps are involved in outputting a piece of work. Every year or so, that number ought to be cut by 30 to 50 percent.

LEADERSHIP LESSONS FOR REDESIGNING THE MODERN AGENCY

✔ Start with the question of core competencies. What are your partners best at? Which services can you provide that are best of class in your field or region?

✔ Come up with a statement that correctly defines the agency's mission and distinguishes it from other marketing services companies in your region.

✔ Go back to your business model and ask how you are going to be adequately paid for your services. Can you package them in such a way as to support top personnel and services in all core areas?

✔ Conduct an internal agency audit at least once a year to determine the efficiency of your company—to wit, how many different steps and people have to touch a piece of work before it becomes a finished ad. What can be done to streamline that process?

✔ Be sure that there are no more than two layers of separation between the senior partners and the lowest person working on any piece of business.

✔ When negotiating fees, analyze the processes on the client side as well. They may be adding additional steps, time, and people to your own production effort. Without involving clients, most reengineering plans are doomed.

✔ Sit down with your clients at least once a year and conduct a brand audit to determine the effectiveness of your communications and all the other services that impact the marketing of a brand. Work with the client to realign the marketing strategy and tactical plans based on such an audit.

✔ If your agency has a strong strategic marketing capability, look at ways to package this work separately from your routine work. One way to do this is to present your client with two media budgets—one for advertising and another for nonadvertising promotions and executions. Another way is to include account service in your

day-to-day advertising budget. Create a separate budget when a
new product is launched or an established brand needs a major
repositioning.

✔ Experiment with ways to retain rights to ideas that have the
potential to be repurposed to other venues or, under certain conditions, to other clients.

✔ Encourage clients to go to others for services that you cannot or do
not want to offer. Where appropriate, help clients in the selection
of those agencies and the integration of their work. Wherever possible, spin off your own below-the-line services into separately
branded companies to ensure their excellence and viability.

CHAPTER 2

The Pitch: Matching the Hatch and Deciding What Would Make the Client Bite Down on Your Lure

When you get to a stream or lake, don't plow right in and start fishing. Better to study the water from a few yards back first and assess the situation. . . . Haphazard casting will get you fish, but a methodical, vacuum-cleaner-like approach will get you more.

Sid Evans
The Trout Fisher's Almanac[1]

As Sid Evans makes clear, if you want to fill your creel in a hurry, you better know how to read the river properly and decide what species of insects your fish are eating. The same deliberate approach is valuable in new business development. Agencies that hit a hot streak are invariably led by people who instinctively know what clients are looking for and can assemble a team capable of delivering insights and ideas on a regular basis. A great idea can win a pitch—but building the sense that over time your agency will be a terrific partner will usually carry the day, even if you aren't able to come up with a winning idea.

To appeal to your prey, you must understand the kind of communications the client is craving. In addition, the lure must appear alive and dynamic. This is a high art that few in the business have mastered. Nor is there any textbook to turn to for instruction. Let's see what we can do to bring this process into focus and suggest some new approaches to increase your win rate.

YOUR PRESENTATION BETTER FIT ON THE FREIGHT ELEVATOR

Jonathan Bond, cofounder of New York hot shop Kirshenbaum Bond & Partners, will always remember the Ace Hardware pitch in the spring of 2002. He and partner Rosemarie Ryan were told to appear at the company's headquarters in Oak Brook, Illinois, at 4 P.M. Kirshen-baum Bond was due to pitch second, directly after Goodby, Silver-stein & Partners of San Francisco, one of the top creative shops in the United States.

The two New Yorkers had brought along a suitcase filled with storyboards (to illustrate their ideas) and cookies (baked in the form of various tools, to lighten up their presentation). They made small talk, watching the elevator for rivals Jeff Goodby and Rich Silver-stein to exit.

At about 10 minutes after four, the elevator door opened and out came several burly workmen pushing two huge TV sets on racks. That indicated Goodby's people had been showing finished work. More workmen appeared delivering huge crates of material. Before long, there were several dozen piles of crates stacked in the reception area.

Finally, after about six elevator trips, Jeff Goodby himself ap-peared, looking fairly pleased, surrounded by a squad of his top peo-ple. Suddenly, Ryan started laughing hysterically, as she and Bond realized they had been totally outgunned—if not in ideas at least in terms of theatrics.

Though Bond and Ryan recovered sufficiently to make a coherent presentation, the account ultimately went to Goodby Silverstein. Perhaps it was because Kirshenbaum Bond failed to project the right cultural fit for the client, or perhaps because their ideas for building Ace Hardware were not as strong as Goodby's. No one save the client will ever know.

"We knew when we entered the room that we had lost," says Bond with good humor, stretching out his legs on a coffee table in his new Soho office. "No matter what we did we couldn't break the spell they had created. Once you are bit by the lovebug, it's pretty much over."

As agencies only exist to serve clients, accounts are the lifeblood of every agency. Strong agencies can be measured by their ability to build revenues from current clients, but often this kind of growth is stunted by factors totally outside the advertising process. Even very good agen-cies have to fuel growth by winning new accounts. Hence the constant emphasis on new business development. Cliff Freeman and Partners, New York, another creative leader, in 2002 saw agency billings fall by half, as first Coca-Cola, then Hardee's, and finally Staples walked out the door. But Freeman never gave up. He threw his efforts into work for current clients like the new sandwich chain, Quiznos, and Mike's Hard Lemonade, then got busy pitching—and winning—accounts like Value City department stores, Designer Shoewear House, and Ben & Jerry's ice cream.

IT ALL STARTS WITH THE RFP

Agencies don't pick their accounts, clients do. The request for proposal (RFP) comes in the form of a questionnaire. At this point, the client is usually playing darts. With or without the help of a consultant, the client has devised a list of 20 or so agencies to consider. Based on submissions, it then narrows the list to a manageable four or five agencies to advance to the next round—a more intense face-to-face meeting.

The requested response to an RFP is usually limited. Most clients just want to know the basics—who your principals are, who your major clients are, what kind of creative and strategic work you've been doing, and a few relevant case histories that demonstrate your ability to work with similar problems or clients. Other addenda, such as the agency's ability to roll out campaigns in distant parts of the world, to develop nonadvertising marketing, and to buy media in a more cost-effective manner, may also be requested. In this early phase, a smart agency will seek to make its submission responsive while also addressing some of the concerns that may be driving the client to seek a new agency in the first place.

The problem with most RFPs is that they don't allow much room for an agency to portray its unique culture or for any kind of direct contact. As in fly-fishing, in the early stages of a pitch an agency must spend time fashioning its lures and make that first cast count. One agency I know sends along a homemade video of its principals talking and joking when it responds to an RFP. It wants to start selling its culture by exposing the client to its people and ambience. Another agency peppers its response with insights gleaned from checking the client's Web site.

If not in this initial stage, then in the first face-to-face meeting, you're going to have to learn how to think like the fish. You want to move from the "Let's get acquainted" process to a discussion of the client's problems. In the initial phase, you're going to score points if you already have a point of view. This takes research. It may force you to play some of your cards before you have had the opportunity to interview people at the brand and hear firsthand how they view their problems.

If you don't have access to client data, send your account planner into the field to study the brand through the eyes of the consumer. One agency head says whenever he got a call from a car client, he didn't immediately return the call. Instead, he would first call several dealers in the field. When he called the client back, he'd open by reviewing the kinds of problems dealers were facing, thus cementing the impression that he was almost as close to the customer and dealers as the client was.

Filling Out the RFP

- Whoa! Are you sure you want to do this? Can you honestly say this business fits the strategic goals of your agency?
- Is the client seriously interested in breaking off its relationship with its current agency, or is this a ghost pitch intended just to scare the hell out of the incumbent?
- What went wrong with the current relationship? Is the client a screamer? Does the client even understand how advertising works? Oh, I see, the client *is* a screamer, but you feel you can reform him or her. Well, if you really believe that, I guess you can skip the rest of this and go on to the next chapter.
- Will the client let you "do famous work," as one Midwestern agency likes to ask?
- Follow the RFP's drift—but not slavishly. Look for ways to customize your response. If the client opens the door by asking why you want to pitch this account, start by indicating your interest in the client's business by reading its annual report, checking out published news accounts, and visiting its Web site. Or better yet, be candid. You're not sure yet whether you want this account, but you want to learn more about the client's business.

- Don't try to anticipate the next phase, the presentation of actual ideas for improving the client's business. Focus at this stage on telling the story of your agency, indicating your experience in this or related fields, providing relevant case histories, and explaining your agency's capabilities. If you get to the next round, there will be time enough for delivering your analysis and ideas.
- Ensure that every question in the RFP is answered. It's amazing how some agencies are so quick to fire up their canned response that they fail to take the time to read the RFP. Most RFPs, though formulaic, have been customized to meet certain special interests of the client. If the client asks whether you're willing to work in an unbundled media environment, you can bet that question isn't there by accident.
- If you don't understand the RFP, call the sender.
- Get it in on time. Clients in general consider agencies to be self-indulgent creative enterprises without a clear understanding of budgets and deadlines. Here's your chance to show that you can tell time.

The last thing to be considered is whether the pitching agency, given the field, has a good chance of winning the account. Virtually no pitch is conducted in secret. The finalists are known. Besides costing tens of thousands of dollars (or, in rare cases, $500,000 or more), pitches use up psychic capital. Losing a high-profile pitch may start an agency on a downward spiral. The loss can demoralize employees and make current clients anxious. The stakes are high. And there can be only one winner.

BE CAREFUL WHAT YOU WISH FOR

As beguiling as new business is to every agency, sometimes it's good to listen to fishing writer Sid Evans: "Better to study the water from a few yards back first and assess the situation." Clients are hungry for solutions—and don't care much, at least on first blush, about the effect of their demands on the agency. One of the first may be to ask you to open an office closer to their headquarters. Though this is a book about becoming more responsive to the new needs of clients, there are limits. Goodby, Silverstein & Partners, GSD&M, Leo Burnett, and The Richards Group, four great U.S. agencies, have declined to open offices beyond their headquarters in the United States because they feel they cannot duplicate the quality of the creative thinking at their home offices. Some agencies embrace account service at the expense of creative services—or vice versa. Some portray themselves as expert at integrating below-the-line marketing services like promotions and direct marketing. Others make it plain they consider integration to be the client's responsibility and try to focus on straight-line advertising.

What is vital is to understand your agency's own unique culture and remain true to it. Certainly there are many reasons to respond to an RFP, but there may be better reasons not to. Agencies need to do a better job of defining who they are. "The cardinal rule we live by," says John Colasanti, president of Minneapolis agency Carmichael Lynch, "is that you are what you eat. In other words, your clients in the end will determine the agency's culture and what it stands for."

Colasanti says that Carmichael Lynch never answers an RFP without first weighing its chances of winning the account, and second, whether the agency could do good work for the client. "Before I worry about what we're going to show and how relevant we are, I want to know what kind of chance we have to win," he says. "Do we know any of their people? What are their backgrounds? Who was the previous agency? We do due diligence to figure out what's going on at the company. We want to get to know them. If we're excited about what we hear, we will definitely go out and talk to them. If we believe there is a possibility of a good fit and if we believe the brand has in it enough texture to work with, then we'll go for it."

WHAT DO YOU SAY ON THE FIRST DATE?

Having decided to pitch, an agency has anywhere from a week to a month to prepare for the crucial first meeting. This is a time of frenzy, because not only must the agency amass great knowledge about the client and its field, it needs to start thinking strategically about the client's business and begin choosing a direction to recommend.

"I view every meeting as a chance to win or lose the business," says Colasanti. "We do a ton of work before we meet prospects. We certainly have an overview of the category and a good analysis of their brand. We conduct a very thorough brand audit. The primary order of business is to talk to the client about their business. It isn't. 'Let's tell you about Carmichael Lynch and we're going to jam three cases down your throat.' Everything we do is going to be tailor-made for the prospect."

"If you go after an account, you're going to have to give it 200 percent," says Jean-Marie Dru, president and CEO of TBWA Worldwide, who, in his days as a leader of Young & Rubicam/Paris and later as cofounder of BDDP, personally led more than 200 pitches. "You will never do enough. When you're 90 percent of the way, you're only one-half of the way. First you have to decide whether to go or not to go—but if you go for it, do twice more than you need to. And always anticipate. You should always be one meeting ahead. When the client's briefing you, you should be asking good questions so you can appear knowledgeable and use such opportunities to collect the information to take you to the next level."

There is considerable debate whether at this meeting you should try to build a vision of your agency to fit what the client is seeking or whether you should be more straightforward and let the chips fall where they may. It's even harder for creatively focused agencies because right away they know the work they're going to present is edgy and will make almost any new client somewhat uneasy. The best advice is to use this occasion to begin building rapport.

Orchestrating the Agency Visit
- To the degree that you can, plan this encounter to ensure that the client has a positive and clear understanding of the agency and its culture.
- Everyone in the agency should know who's visiting and when. If they have a chance meeting with the visitor, they should know enough about the account to make an intelligent comment.
- The walk-through should be fun, fast, and in no way complete.

There is no reason, for instance, to show prospects the accounting department or the traffic department. Seeing the creative department and one other work area should be enough.

- Thought should go into decorating the lobby and the conference room in which you're going to be talking to the client. The lobby should reflect the culture and standard of work of the agency. The conference room should be a comfortable, clean meeting area. The more of your work on the walls the better, but otherwise don't put much emphasis on window dressing.

- Unless you've scheduled a noon meeting, you don't need to set up an elaborate buffet. Soft drinks, bottled water, fresh coffee, and munchies are enough.

- People should be relaxed and prepared. This is basically a credentials presentation. You're going to want to find out what you can about the client's interests, introduce the client to some of your top people, and lay down one or two relevant case histories to show how you work.

- Show an interest in the client's business, but unless the client specifically asks for it ahead of time, don't feel you have to use this meeting to expose the client to a strategic or advertising idea.

- Clients are people. Use common sense in welcoming them as you would any guest. Listen carefully to their questions or comments. If you don't have an answer, send it to them later. Don't grovel, but try to start making connections. The pitch process is a rare opportunity to have the client alone and ready to talk. What you can learn on this visit will help you prepare for the next session.

- Try to avoid PowerPoint presentations. Whatever rapport was building may be destroyed by someone reading slides from a screen. Clients want to know what you're made of, both personally and as a creative center. Your mission, your processes, your client list and billings—all these things can be addressed in written submissions. One or two case histories are appropriate, but keep them brief and to the point.

- The more interactive you can make this meeting, the better.

"Disruption is a powerful concept which we're proud to embrace," says Lee Clow of TBWA Chiat/Day. "When we go in to pitch a piece of business, we're trying to establish a relationship on the basis of our intellectual talents, not just our creativity.

"At the same time, we're also selling the notion that if you don't push the envelope, that if you don't do something that's strategically disruptive, the brand is going to remain in the same place. What we try to bring to the table is an idea that lets you leap over what the competition is, and so we put our brave thinking in the context of a business strategy before we ever show ads that might be a little scary or different than what a client thinks they should be.

"In new business, you are trying to create trust, but still hopefully on the terms [that will make the client conclude] these guys are so smart and have such an interesting way of thinking about my business problem, as well as having them do advertising . . . they could be an asset to my company."

Clow counsels being true to your agency's belief system. "Presentation gurus come in and say, 'Basically you have to figure out who the client is and then turn your agency into what he wants to hire.' I think that's bullshit," he says, with characteristic bluntness. "We go in and try to understand the client in terms of his needs and his wants and who is his audience. We try to show them how we think about the business and how we think about the advertising they should do. So if we get hired, we get hired for the right reasons. And if we don't get hired, it's because they didn't want what we sell."

Others say that matchmaking requires personal chemistry, and agencies would do well to design their new business team to fit the culture of the client. "Basically the whole thing is about tailoring," says Jonathan Bond. "Without the tailoring, a suit doesn't fit. If you don't do any tailoring, you don't make any connections. Tonality is more important than creative content. We've been in pitches where the client said we did not having the winning strategy, but we won the account anyway.

"I remember one account, Beech-Nut [the baby-food maker]," says Bond. "They all came from St. Louis. We were New Yorkers, of course. The protocol called for a social meeting and then a business meeting. Normally, you would go out to a restaurant with them. But I said, 'You're all coming to my house for dinner.' My girlfriend suggested we do baby food—baby carrots, baby lamb chops. It was fabulous. Next day we had the meeting. The meeting bombed. They hated the idea we presented. And we still won the business. In the end they just liked us."

Ideas count. Clients are looking for an agency experienced at attacking the kind of problems they face—as well as ideas on how to build their brand. Then, too, selecting an agency depends on whether a company thinks its marketing department and the agency make a good team.

Michael Agate, founder of the powerful Los Angeles–based search consultancy, Select Resources International, stresses the importance of chemistry. He even writes out formal "chemistry checks" for the client to fill out after each meeting—with points like, "Did they have a respectful collaborative style that will engage our participation?" and "Do we feel good about the chemistry and respect their team?"

NOW YOU'VE DONE IT, OLLIE—YOU GOT US INVITED TO THE PARTY

Some clients approach the first meeting in a casual manner—figuring this is just an opportunity to get acquainted and go over the points raised in the credentials presentation. Typically, no decisions are made in this instance, or at least not consciously. Others may be in a hurry to move the pitch along and start seeing ideas in the hopes of beginning to narrow the list of finalists.

The first challenge for an agency is to get properly briefed on what is expected of it in this first face-to-face meeting and form an appropriate team for the task. If the meeting is to have a fairly light tone, agencies can plan on spending more time introducing their people, talking about their philosophy, and interacting with the client team. But many agencies—thinking along the lines of Jean-Marie Dru's stricture to "*Anticipate! Anticipate!*"—want to use this meeting to begin pointing the client toward a strategy. Some agencies even bring finished ideas to the meeting. That's probably a risky approach. However, there seems to be a consensus that the first horse out of the gate may win the race, so it's hard to avoid the urge to move things along.

IDEAS ARE THE CROWN JEWELS

Ideas are in the title of this book. They are the Holy Grail of advertising. Sometimes an idea does not lead directly to an advertising strategy but may be more of a general positioning or marketing strategy. Sometimes the idea is in fact an advertising line—and so powerful it will drive the advertising and the business strategy for years to come. "Think Different," was such a line for Apple and helped to set the stage for Steve Jobs's later introduction of the iMac. "Solutions for a Small Planet," from Ogilvy & Mather repositioned IBM as a company devoted to becoming more customer-focused, thus helping Louis Gerstner and his managers transform the company from a Wall Street disaster back into a world leader.

Such ideas are valuable, but agencies bemoan the fact that they are asked for them in the midst of contests to win a piece of business and that they have little chance of protecting such intellectual capital or getting properly paid for it—unless they are fortunate enough to win the pitch.

Lee Clow of TBWA Chiat/Day deplores the inequity of pitches. "It's very demeaning that we have to put on a show to prove that we know how to put on a show," Clow says, over a breakfast of fruit and bagels in his ground-floor office at TBWA Chiat/Day's new Playa del Rey headquarters. "Even though we've got evidence galore that we know how to do a certain thing, we still have to go in and dance and sing and do cartwheels.

"It's very, very frustrating that we have to give away what we do. The type of strategic rigor we go through and the analysis that we bring to the table when we do a pitch is what these damn consulting firms walk in and charge $1 million for. And we do it for free so that we can set the stage to show them some ads that might propel their marketing forward.

"I think we still have more collective brainpower in our industry than some of the other industries that have been showcased, whether it's consulting or the interactive companies which for a moment in time were going to eclipse all the advertising companies. I think our brainpower is immense, and we have to give it away on a regular basis to win a new account."

Clow admits that the practice of clients expecting to be served up free ideas at this stage is unlikely to change. The effort to give away some great ideas in exchange for the chance to win a piece of business will continue for the foreseeable future.

WHERE DO THESE WINNING IDEAS COME FROM?

Great strategic thinking grows out of deep knowledge of a brand and its category. Insights come from a close study of the consumer, the competitive set in the category, the heritage and equities of a brand, and the vagaries of the marketplace—or any combination of these elements. A brilliant planner can sometimes divine such insights in a matter of hours or days. But often this process takes weeks or months. Usually, presenters only have a few weeks to complete preparations for this first meeting, so they're going to have to drill down quickly into the problem and then make some critical decisions.

Lee Clow's Approach to Pitching
- The intensity of a pitch is perhaps the most fun there is in advertising. Encourage the camaraderie and teamwork that goes into making a pitch successful. Even if you lose, you want your team to feel they had a good time working their butts off.
- Don't spend too much time trying to figure out what the client wants to hear. Figure out what you have to tell them.
- Tell the truth about your agency. If you're a hot creative shop, don't try to hide it. You want to be sure you're hired for the right reasons—otherwise, the relationship is never going to work.
- Present only ideas you love and believe in. Every idea you present should be something you wouldn't mind doing, not just for a few months but for a few years.
- Look for ways to make the client comfortable with your agency. Showing you are good listeners may be more important than showing you are good talkers.
- If you're going to show disruptive work, take the time to give it the context of a business strategy. It's not disruptive for the fun of it—it's disruptive because it's smart.

- Advertising that maintains the status quo is going to leave the client company in the same place it was yesterday. Disruptive advertising might seem scary or different at first, but it's scary for a reason. It's going to let the brand leap over the competition. Take time to show how this will happen.
- People with disruptive ideas don't have to be jerks. Be smart and good and intelligent—not arrogant—but if the client is going to dictate the advertising, maybe you don't belong in the room.

There is the idea you need to win the business and then the idea the client needs to get back into the game. Ideally, they are one and the same. But often they are not. A pitching agency has to decide how blunt to be with the client in talking about its brands—and what strategy to recommend. Jean-Marie Dru has worked with food maker Danone as a client since 1984 and recalls the difficulty in making decisions early in a pitch on what line to take.

"In a pitch, you never have enough time," Dru says, taking a quick lunch in his sparsely furnished TBWA office in New York after his arrival on the morning Air France flight from Paris. "In the first week you do a lot. You have to build knowledge and plan everything very fast. It's then up to the team leader, whoever that person is, to be responsible for the idea that will decide whether you win or you lose. Are we going to recommend A or B? If you don't decide anything, your presentation won't be very good because you have no commitment.

"Take Danone. They are doing yogurt and dessert. The first one is good for health, the second one perhaps not so good. So do you want to have a health strategy or not? The decision between indulgence and health is a big decision. If you ask me what is the most important thing for that business, I think it is for the client is to find the right balance between those two values. And it will be different in each country. But someone has to decide."

THE THEATRICS OF A GOOD PITCH

Jeff Goodby, certainly one of the maestros of new business casting, thinks pitching is more about chemistry than ideas. "Most agencies go into a pitch and think what will win the day is coming up with a great idea. And wowing the client. I tell my people all the time, 'You've got to have a great idea and you've got to have great work, but what it's really about is whether they like you as people and want to hang around with you.' Because even if you don't have such a powerful idea on the day of the pitch, if you can convince them you have the ability to come up with it, they'll hire you."

Goodby believes in most cases it's nearly impossible to come up with such an idea in the three or four weeks between the credentials process and the final shootout. "A lot of winning pitches come when clients like you and your people like each other," he says. "This sounds crazy, but your people have to really show they like working together. I've been in pitches, especially back in the early days, when there was some open friction over what we were presenting or how we felt about it. That really is the worst possible scenario.

"So we spend a lot of time trying to create an environment in the room that everyone will want to take part in. That's why we bring all that stuff. We look at the room, and if the room is cold, ugly, no fun— we actually come up with a way to redecorate the room and surround people with the work that we're showing or that's relevant to what we're pitching. People respond to that. They think, 'This is an environment I want to hang around in.' "

Goodby says he sends scouts to measure the presentation room and videotape it and then he and his top people try to decide how they can make it a better theater for their work. "The room is part of the environment," he says. "Your people have to feel comfortable and the client has to feel comfortable in it. A lot of people think it's not important, and they're wrong. Especially when these clients are auditioning five really smart agencies. It makes a big difference for them to walk back into that same room for our pitch, and suddenly it's transformed.

"When we pitched Sega a few years ago, they wanted us to use a certain room at a Holiday Inn. It was a big ballroom kind of place. We got covering for the walls, brought in bleachers—brought every person from the agency to the pitch. They walked in and we were all sitting there. And weeks before the pitch, we assigned every person in the agency a Sega game to learn. So everybody in the agency was a specialist in one of their games.

"First, having all the people in the agency there showed we had a lot of enthusiasm for this piece of business. Second, it showed our own people how we pitched things, which was really a fascinating learning process for them. And third, I was able to turn to Sega and say: 'Right up there is a specialist in every one of the games that you make. We have somebody that knows it, that has been playing it days and nights, right down to the stupidest, worst games that you make. Even the ones that hardly sell at all.'

"That was very powerful. Video games are all about sound and light. So we got nine television sets and stacked them, three by three. We got an engineer and made those nine screens into one. There was one enormous screen up in front made out of nine boxes. When Sega people walked in, they saw a teenager playing one of their games. And for a sound system we had hired a club system that The Grateful Dead used. It was loud as hell. It was like Desert Storm.

"All our people were wearing Sega jackets and clothes. I have videotapes of this pitch and look back on it now and then and think, 'That was a really fun day.' We had people dressed as Sega game characters. I mean, it was really wacky. But the sum total is that while I can't remember some of the work we presented, we knew we got across the message that 'These guys would be really fun to hang around with' and of course we won the business."

Jeff Goodby's Rules for Smart Pitching

- Ideas are great. But if you can't come up with a great idea, at least come up with a great feeling.
- Your people are your agency's best reference. Think about ways of making them comfortable so that they can enjoy themselves and project good vibes.
- Scout the room. Figure out how you can turn it into a creative environment, if just for 60 minutes. Assume that all the pitches the client hears that day are going to sound the same. What's going to stick in the client's mind is the feeling that he or she had listening to your pitch. That can be determined as much as by how your people act and how the room looks as by what you say.

- Talk, and leave time for questions so that the client gets to talk.
- Pay attention to what's going on during the pitch. Even the smallest comment should be heard. Don't be shy about reacting to what's said or altering your script of the pitch to respond. In fact, to the degree possible, arrange your script to allow for that kind of flexibility.
- If you don't think you're going to like working with the client, don't go. If someone is not on board, leave them behind. Clients pick up more on the way you and your people interact with each other than on what you say.
- Have a good time pitching. In fact, have a good time in advertising or do something else. Life is too short not to have fun.

KNOW HOW TO READ THE ROOM

Goodby will always remember the Alaska Airlines pitch. His agency's design studio had been intrigued with finding just the right leave-behind to clinch the win. In this case, according to Goodby, his people got carried away.

"They decided to make a flight bag out of brushed aluminum, with leather straps and the emblem of Alaska Airlines embossed into it. And when you opened it up, it had all this wonderful stuff from the Northwestern part of the United States that would be interesting if you were traveling on Alaska Airlines. You had socks from Pendleton Mills, coffee from Starbucks, stuff from Eddie Bauer, and so on. It was just astonishingly cool.

"But when we got in there, the CEO came in. We'd not met him before. And he gave a little speech about how bad things were at the airline financially. Southwest was killing them and Alaska was having to cut back on everything, laying people off and cutting back on the frills. And we went, 'Holy shit, we can't pass out those leave-behinds, because he's going to think this is just an extravagant waste of money.' I remember passing a note back to Silverstein saying we're screwed. When the note hit the designer, Paul Curtin, all the blood drained out of his face. He and his people had worked so hard on the cases for weeks."

REMEMBER, YOU DON'T NEED TO FILL
THE TIME BLOCK

Agencies are usually given 90 minutes for their presentation. In actuality, though, that leaves less than 60 minutes to make your points, because you have to leave time for questions. A good presenter wants to throw two or three case histories into the mix, talk about the agency's early insights into the brand, and begin hinting at solutions. After introducing the rest of the team—and letting each member have about five minutes to talk about their own capabilities—the hour is easily gone.

In many ways, agencies would do well to script even less than that. If Mike Agate is right that these meetings are as much about chemistry as ideas, then presenters should keep their points short and use most of the time to smoke out the client's sensitivities and mold their presentation around them. Everyone dreads a PowerPoint presentation where the speaker reads every slide. Clients are human. They come with their own baggage. Start drawing them out. Think on your feet, or better yet, come prepared with answers to anything that might come up, and you will no doubt pass to the next round.

"If we have a 60-minute meeting, we leave 30 minutes to just talk," says Colasanti. "We might design key points in the meeting where we stop and open it up. Because we view this as a chance to get to know the prospect and for the prospect to see us thinking on our feet. We engage in chemistry from the get-go. As the pitch develops it may be more strictly choreographed, so we work as much dialogue as possible into these early meetings. If along the way we see an opportunity to get to know these people, we do. Otherwise, we're spending the bulk of our time coming up with the smartest recommendation we can."

Bob Schmidt, the cofounder of the former New York creative shop, Levine Huntley Schmidt & Beaver, usually missed the first credentials presentation. The next day, he would phone, requesting a private session with the client. He would then travel to the client's headquarters and, in a valuable one-on-one session, begin to establish a personal relationship and gain insights into the client's business problems.

"Inevitably, the client will tell you his 'truths,' " Schmidt says. "He knows his brand better than you ever will. He knows the competition. He knows the marketplace. I would get four-hour lunches where they told me about their wives or husbands, their children, their business. The client tells you everything you need to know. If you sit there, and you don't spill food on your tie, and you're nice and intelligent, they start to relate to you. By the end of that meeting, I was so far into their heads that if we merely did something as smart as everybody else we were likely going to get the account."

Jonathan Bond recalls pitching Ikea. "The first thing we did— everyone in the room brought along their baby pictures. You had to guess who was who. So it was immediately interactive and fun," he says. The tendency in a credentials presentation is to talk *at* a client. "The trick is to get them to interact," says Bond. "Remember, most people don't start out caring about you—they care about themselves. They're thinking. 'Do I like these guys?' So what you have to do is say, 'Here's our clients. We have retailers just like you. We have seven people in the style business who are up on the latest trends.' You have to find the connections before the chemistry can get started."

LET THEM FALL IN LOVE WITH YOU
AND YOUR IDEAS

Mary Wells, Jeff Goodby, and the other expert new business pitchers emphasize that the exercise is part theater. Your purpose is to create a 60-minute encounter so enthralling that the account will be virtually handed to you on a platter. Successful agencies learn how to inject a sense of fun into their presentations. Ideas can usually be communicated very quickly. The rest of the meeting should be about making connections.

Schmidt recalls pitching the $40 million Frito-Lay account. He assembled a creative team, an account person, a planner, and a media specialist—along with Don Peppers, one of the legendary rainmakers of the 1980s.[2]

"We weren't on their list at all," Schmidt recalls. "Don did something at the last minute to get their attention. Typically, it was something unusual—sending flags, banners, life-size cutouts, or a Mercedes limo to pick them up. Whatever it took, he got us in.

"These guys walked in and said, 'You have half an hour.' We had been preparing for this meeting out the window. We understood the product, we understood the business, we had all been in the stores, we talked to store managers, we talked to scores of truck drivers. The drivers knew what their problems were. They're in the stores every day, pushing other products off their facings and fighting for every sale.

"We came to them and did a series of vignettes—acted them out ourselves. We showed that this was a product that parents gave to their kids to keep them happy. If you could convince mothers chips would give them some peace with their kids, you were home free. The half an hour became an hour and then three hours. They left at 5:00 in the evening. The head guy, Leo Kiley, put his arm around me and said, 'We'll be back.' Monday morning we got a call that we had won the account. We just hit them, the chemistry was wonderful, we understood what they wanted to accomplish, we gave them comic relief. We showed them that people don't eat these products for nutrition—they eat them while they're having fun. And we gave them a tremendously happy environment to put the product in."

The other thing many clients are looking for is a unique idea. It's very hard for agencies to happen on this in just two or three weeks. The simplest way for anyone new to a brand to sense where the brand should move would be to get the strategy from the client. But it is unlikely in a competitive pitch that clients will do the thinking for an agency. Anyway, the client might be wrong. It may have been misdirection from the client that caused the advertising to go awry in the first place. You have to work independently to validate the client's strategy and research.

Increasingly, the pressure has been for the account planner to come up with the insight. "Planning is everything now," says Tracy Wong, cofounder of WONGDOODY, a Seattle-based hot shop with offices in Los Angeles and Dallas. "By the time planner is done talking, the work is usually sold. In pitches, you're usually selling a difficult idea. Planning sets the stage. With a good planner, the idea just drops into place. Sometimes you can almost hear it click."

"Because of the time line," says Kirshenbaum Bond's Rosemarie Ryan, "we actually start the planning process as soon as we know we're in the pitch. You have to believe you're going to get through to the next round—and it's good because when you get to the credentials part of the presentation you're not just talking about yourself. If you can talk about the client that early, you start to build better rapport."

Planning means studying the brand, its advertising, consumers, and the competition and understanding the role it does or can play in the world. "We don't wait until we have the brief before we engage the creatives" says Ryan. "I don't believe in the factory line kind of thing. I don't think it works. We start working with creative people from the beginning, sharing with them our thoughts and our learning. So that by the time creative people get briefed—they're pretty familiar with what is the problem and what point of view we have for solving that strategic problem."

"We have to believe, 'He who thinks the best wins,'" says Carmichael Lynch's Colasanti. "Otherwise, you get all tangled up. Maybe we aren't as good on the relationship front or in political navigation as some agencies. So it's more about applying ourselves and hoping that we win through our work."

When you think you know the problem, only then can you start coming up with solutions. The ideas that will solve the brief are relatively easy if you have a precise, accurate brief. If you're off-kilter in your perception of the problem—if you've moved too quickly or sloppily through the analysis phase—then your solution is probably going to be off-kilter, too. In that case, only great chemistry can save you.

There are debates about whether to present one idea or many. Some agencies feel more comfortable showering the client with several ideas—just to show how energetic and quick on their feet they are. Others present a single idea to show their belief in a single strategy that they believe best solves the brand challenge of the moment. There is no textbook answer.

In the end, make your best pitch, answer the client's questions, pack up your presentation, and go somewhere relaxing and wait for the decision. Many agency heads say they know early on when they've lost a pitch. Others insist you can never be sure: Regardless of what your gut is telling you, you need to give it your best shot.

You may have the jitters. The fast food you wolfed down at lunch may be burning a hole in your stomach. You may realize that telling your people not to dress up for the meeting was a mistake. You may be blindsided by the sudden appearance of the CEO or a decision maker you didn't even know existed. It doesn't matter. By the time you come to all these nervous conclusions, it's too late. You've committed your troops. You've arrayed your team in battle. All you can do is attack and hope for the best.

Returning to my fly-fishing metaphor, I've often appeared at a promising turn in the river at the right time of day with what others said was just the right gear. My casts were near perfect—given where the fish ought to be feeding. By all I could determine from what insects were feeding at that season, I believed my lure was right. But I would cast and cast and cast, and nothing would bite. Then, the next day, someone fishing that same river, with the same lure or even one less appropriate, would land a 12-pounder on the first cast. There's no explaining failure one day and success another. But ask yourself this: Were you smart enough to make this cast in the first place? Did you have the experience, the knowledge, and the tackle the river required? If you can't answer yes, then it's time to withdraw and refit your whole new business process.

DON'T EXPECT TO FISH .500 ALL THE TIME

Winning two pitches out of ten is considered a pretty good record. If you're not winning *any*, then of course you have to regroup. If you're winning more than 20 percent, consider yourself very lucky.

"At the end of day, it's chemistry" says Jean-Marie Dru. "People always forget that. This industry has a lot of stupid, arrogant people who believe they are smarter than the other guys and that smarter is the way you get new business. You don't. You get new business because you show the client you're going to be a great partner. We're a very creative agency. So our work is going to create discomfort in someone seeing it for the first time. We know that. So we try to build comfort between ourselves and the client. The more creative you are, the harder that is."

LEADERSHIP LESSONS FOR SUCCESSFUL PITCHING

✔ Be careful what you pitch. Remember, every new account has the potential to change your agency—for good or ill.

✔ Know why you're in the pitch. Time is money. Just getting through round one will cost the agency in terms of energy and time taken away from other business. In every pitch there are more losers than winners—and the losers often pay a psychic price.

✔ Be ready to throw everything you have into a pitch. In the days or weeks between turning in the RFP and the credentials presentation, the agency must make sure it knows all it can about the client, the product, the history of its advertising, the category and the consumer mind-set. Where are the openings? How can the brand grow? Where does it need to defend? And so on. Getting brand insights takes time. Give your planning department as much support as possible. Their insights may take you to the next round.

✔ Don't be in a hurry to produce spec creative. If the client demands it, let the idea, not the execution, shine through. Make a strategic call about whether you want to present one idea or several. If you do present more than one to show off your versatility, make sure you know what you consider the right idea for the client—and be ready to defend it.

✔ Take your time trying to get to know the client personally at the highest level possible before the pitch.

✔ Leave plenty of time. Even in facing a large room of people, take your time introducing your people and doing what you can to make their personalities come alive. Let the character of your people and your agency shine. Chemistry sometimes is more important than any single idea.

✔ Try to scout the room ahead of time and think about what you can do to make it feel like the inside of your agency. Think about making your people comfortable. If they are at ease, their enthusiasm will be an important ingredient to getting an edge.

✔ Tell the truth about your agency. You may believe you're everything any client could ever want, but get an outside opinion and
try to be objective. Agencies are living, breathing social organ-
isms. Clients know this. Don't fake it. Admit your weaknesses and
turn them into strengths.

✔ Understand the brief. If possible, get the client's reading of the
brief first. Then have your planners check it out. If you believe the
brief is wrong, say so. If the client won't change it, then either
pitch the brief or get out of the pitch.

✔ When presenting an idea, remember that media placement may
be more important than the creative. Try to be media-neutral. If
an idea can be expressed just as well by sticking labels on fruit in
markets as by putting it up on billboards, say so. If sponsoring
beach volleyball will have more impact than a print campaign in
Rolling Stone, go to the beach.

CHAPTER 3

Creative Department: How Long Can It Survive as Idea Central?

Fishermen are a perverse and restless lot, constantly poised to migrate to greener pastures, ever helpless recruits for the wild goose chase.

Roger Traver
Trout Madness[1]

Creativity has achieved an iconic status in the advertising world. Creatives are allowed to come to work in running shoes and jeans, wear their hair long, and install pool tables and basketball hoops in their work areas. Agencies pamper them with pizza and Chinese food when they work late, and many reward their best creatives with expensive, weeklong trips to distant festivals in places like Cannes and South Beach to keep their creative juices flowing.

Typically, they hang out together or with creatives from other disciplines or, worse, from other agencies. Some arrive late for meetings and fail to turn in time sheets. They are a perverse and restless lot, always worried about what is happening down the hall or across the street—bellyaching about conditions in their own agency and dreaming of taking a higher-paying position somewhere else. But all is forgiven as long as they come up with a breakthrough campaign that impresses the client and saves the business. Is there anything wrong with this scenario? Not really—it's just that what's considered a breakthrough idea is about to change, and most creative departments are not equipped to handle the need for new kinds of thinking.

"The advertising industry is the most conservative industry in the world," says Keith Reinhard, chairman of DDB Worldwide and a former copywriter and creative director himself. "And ironically, within the agency, those most resistant to change are the creative people."

It's not that agencies don't celebrate creativity. Marketing communications is basically a creative process—requiring at times a suspension of disbelief to test out a counterintuitive idea that in the end may dramatically boost a brand. The elevation of the creative makes perfect sense. But without radical change, its value to the agency will decrease. Classically speaking, these people have been trained and organized to do ads. Ads have their place—but in the new marketing era, they won't always carry the day.

The issue is not whether creative people should see their work and position as exalted, but at what cost and for what reason. If they can expand their role to include the new media-neutral culture that clients are embracing, then their canonization is justified. But if they do not evolve to fill the void that now exists, then their role will be taken over by other disciplines.

Advertisers are already learning to look elsewhere for ideas. Just as we've seen media unbundled and shopped out to media-only companies, creative services may be shopped out—as has happened with Coca-Cola over the past decade. Clients have come to see agencies as factories that make ads. Clients suspect agencies of trying to sell them ads—either because their compensation is tied to media placement or because agencies don't know any other trade. That is about to change.

TIME TO REACH INTO THE FLY BOX

Change may start with recruiting a new type of creative—a creative planner, if you will, instead of a copywriter or an art director. But there are no schools for creative planners, and the job really doesn't exist right now.

"Agencies have to develop a new kind of person," says Jeff Goodby, cofounder of Goodby, Silverstein & Partners in San Francisco, one of the most honored creative agencies in the world. "And I don't know what to call them. Maybe it's a kind of supercharged version of creatives who understand media a bit and who are able to step back and say, 'Let's do something different. Let's project laser work onto buildings. Let's put an enormous yellow sticky on the Golden Gate Bridge.' That's the kind of thinking that we're going to have come up with in the future."

Nick Brien, new business development leader for Starcom MediaVest, would call this new kind of creative a *brand architect*. "We need liberating, redefining brand ideas in whatever form. At the moment, most conventional agencies are structured that way because most creatives come from advertising," says Brien.

"That's their world, that's what they know, that's what they want to do. I say that without undermining the role of agencies; we now need an idea-generation trust that knows how to work as a team. Somewhat like architects. An architect has to be able to imagine the idea of a building and has to be able to create a framework for it. The architect has to be responsible for creating something enduring, powerful, and relevant. It has to be successful and functional in the ultimate construction."

ISN'T JOB ONE MAKING GREAT ADS?

In this new Age of Aquarius, it's going to be important for agencies to redefine the mission of the whole creative department. There will be times when brands are best served by traditional ads and collateral. At other times, an event or a radical new use of ambient media may offer better opportunities. Agencies are either going to have to retrain their creative directors in these nonadvertising arts or develop a new supercreative, as Goodby suggested, who can determine when to present nonadvertising ideas to the client.

We could see yet another department developed to accommodate them—a "brand happening" department aligned with promotions or event planning or PR. But if agencies did that under current rules, the effort would be marginalized. Agency leaders have to make a greater commitment than that. Bob Schmetterer, cofounder of Messner Vetere Berger McNamee Schmetterer Euro RSCG in New York and now chairman and CEO of Euro RSCG Worldwide, has refocused his whole advertising network to come up with Creative Business Ideas™ (CBIs)—and has even trademarked the phrase.[2]

"Creative Business Ideas™ may involve advertising but they aren't the same as advertising," says a Euro RSCG new-business publication. "Advertising has habitually been used as the primary means of building relationships between consumers and brands. With Creative Business Ideas™, we are breaking that habit. And as a measure of our confidence in breaking the advertising habit, we are bold enough to say in some cases: Do not do any advertising.

"Advertising is wonderful. It's one of our tools. But it's only one tool, suitable for certain types of jobs. Remember the old saying: 'To a man with a hammer, every problem looks like a nail.' There are plenty more tools and plenty more jobs. Put your hammer down!"[3]

Schmetterer has organized an annual competition to honor the best two or three CBIs within his global network. He is unusual in this effort.[4] The closest other agency networks have come to Schmetterer's CBI competition is to add an internal global Effie contest to their own internal creative competitions. Right now the awareness of how business-transforming ideas are more important than business-building advertising hasn't registered.

"I've felt for a long time that the unique reason for being in this industry is to think creatively," says Schmetterer. "Not just thinking analytically or strategically but creatively. That's what sets us apart from the big consultancies—applying creativity to our client's businesses at the highest level. Our ideas for our clients should be more transcendant than just saying you need a new campaign for the fall."

GETTING CLOSE TO THE CLIENT

As the palette of creative directors expands and the tools at their disposal increase, some may find themselves actually getting closer to clients. This is not a bad thing. The problem with clients today is that they suspect agencies of being interested only in increasing revenue. And they suspect creative directors—who in the current environment often have supplanted account executives as presenters—of trying to sell them ads.

In a few instances, this change is already happening. Steve Hayden, a creative giant in the 1980s and 1990s and part of the team at Chiat/Day that developed the "1984" commercial introducing the Macintosh and later built BBDO/West into a leading office, eventually moved to Ogilvy & Mather, where for seven years he served as "president" of the $400 million global IBM account. Today, he is vice chairman of the agency.

On Hayden's watch Ogilvy came up with the enduring "Solutions for a small planet." His team developed the distinctive blue-bordered e-business campaign as Gerstner refocused IBM on selling services and consulting and not just hardware and broadened its mandate to serve small and medium-size businesses, not just giants.

At Goodby, three creative directors have taken over an alpha dog role on agency accounts: Steve Simpson for both the Hewlett-Packard and Compac accounts, Jamie Barrett on Saturn, and Harry Cocciolo on SBC and Discover. Their elevation has caused account service people to report to them—simply because clients have bonded with the creative directors and trust their recommendations more than anyone else at the agency.

"Watching these three in everyday life," says Goodby, "you realize they are a combination of account person and creative director. I do that all the time, myself." This evolution, Goodby notes, has changed the way creatives see themselves and the role they play on accounts. Though Goodby does not plan to give these alpha dog creative leaders new titles (because he feels creatives won't entrust their nascent ideas to anyone outside the creative department), he does feel creatives at the agency must understand that one of their new responsibilities is to be able to sell their ideas directly to clients.

"The old days of a creative person being some kind of brooding, client-hating, noncommunicative character are over. Those guys don't work that well in this job anymore," says Goodby. "You can have creative people who have entirely different points of view from anybody else in the world. They don't have to be liked, but they have to be able to communicate."

Leading a brand at a forward-looking agency isn't just a communication challenge; it's also a question of being comfortable with working in a media-neutral landscape. To do that, creative departments may have to recruit people with much more exotic backgrounds—those whose training extends well outside the portfolio curriculum for copywriters and art directors.

Having assembled a more eclectic team, the new creative department chief will then have to reorganize the process in which ideas are assembled and cooked. Where previously there were shootouts to come up with advertising ideas, the competition has to be opened up to anything that will move the brand deeper into the culture and generate interest.

I would call this process an *idea rodeo*. Calf roping is fine, but bull-dogging may be better. There's no limit to how many ideas an agency presents, but there is a hierarchy. Presenters have to be prepared to weigh ideas for importance and potential. Often, all of this will have to come out of the advertising budget, which may be fixed for the fiscal or calendar year. Clients want to be told not only where the brand *can* go but where it *should* go.

CREATIVITY THE IDEO WAY

For a model of how to organize your own brand rodeo, you need to look no further than IDEO in Palo Alto, California, one of the leading product design firms. IDEO, in its relatively short, 24-year lifespan, has turned out an astonishing list of exciting products—everything from the first standup toothpaste tube (for Procter & Gamble) to the Palm V organizer to the interior of the Amtrak's high-speed Acela trains to Apple's iPod music player. In the past decade, in *BusinessWeek*'s annual Industrial Design Excellence Awards, the magazine has cited IDEO designs 58 times—almost double the awards of its nearest competitor.

IDEO employs various idea-generating techniques, which are all described in general manager Tom Kelley's book, *The Art of Innovation*. (See Appendix C.) The firm has been described as a "creativity factory" with about 350 people working in 20 studios around the world. Kelley believes "innovation begins with the eye," so designers are initially expected to observe consumers either firsthand or in filmed focus groups.

Following this, teams work on design problems and attend brainstorming sessions in which participants are encouraged to come up with silly ideas and exchange random thoughts. On the walls of the brainstorming conference rooms are signs that say, "Go for quantity," "Encourage wild ideas," "Defer judgment," and "One conversation at a time." Kelley's creativity factory is not in a hurry to form a brief. He quotes Nobel prize winner Linus Pauling, "The best way to get a good idea is to get a lot of ideas." At the end of this process, one idea emerges as the preferred application, and it is moved to a more concrete stage where it starts to take shape, either on the drawing board or in scale models.

The typical agency creative process today is quite different. Profiling consumers is usually the job of account planners, trained specialists who observe people using the product and view the advertising of the brand and its competitors. They come back and relate their findings to the creative department—in some cases, even go so far as to map the brand's equities and provide insights on how the brand can evolve. From this a brief is drafted, often with account management and client input, and then handed to a creative team, usually consisting of a copywriter and art director, who are supposed to translate it into an ad campaign. The team is encouraged to come up with several ideas, which a creative director or creative review committee may winnow down to a single thought. Seldom are creatives encouraged to break out of the advertising box and play with nonadvertising ideas that might provide a more powerful communication platform for the brand and have a greater impact.

MAKING CONTENT COMPELLING

In addition to being under pressure now to think more broadly, agencies are on notice that in the future they are going to have to launch and defend brands in a much more unfriendly media environment. Consumers are developing stronger filters to protect themselves against poorly presented communications; meanwhile, the media environment is so fragmented that it's getting harder and harder to catch someone's attention—let alone drive home a message. Some practitioners believe agencies will have to become more skilled at devising compelling content that won't feel like advertising at all.

"Long-form branded content is already here," says DDB's Keith Reinhard. "We're producing material right now for the new Channel BOB [Brief Original Broadcasts]. This is a new cable channel which will present up to eight segments an hour—three of which can be 'commercials'—but they must be so entertaining people will choose to watch them. To make sure they are, Channel BOB has an editorial board that must approve any branded content. If you don't get past the editorial board, you don't get on the channel. This is good because it forces us to come up with branded content that is entertaining."

New technologies like TiVo have begun to enable consumers to eliminate advertising from TV altogether. Moreover, research shows that consumers are increasingly irritated by the some 2,000 to 3,000 commercial messages they see each day. According to one recent survey, fully 74 percent of people in the prime 30 to 44 age group feel that "advertising is now in far too many places; you can't get away from it."[5] As advertising is perceived as more of a nuisance, consumers are developing new psychic filters to tune it out.

Content will be so engaging that consumers will either welcome the interruption, as they have with the Absolut campaign, or may even begin to seek out commercials as a form of entertainment.

"With TiVo, people have to be drawn to advertising and want to see it," says Jeff Goodby. "We're not going to be able to get them to watch advertising against their will. There may be instances where people will have to watch a spot first to get to the content they want to see on the Web, much as TV does now. But the real future is to have an ad on TV running on your Internet site at a certain hour of the day and you will advertise when it will appear, just like a movie. I think the new Nike 'Tag' commercial, for instance, is so good it could be on prime time, and people would actually tune in to see it."

This was the strategy Fallon followed in developing BMW films for BMW. The agency proposed making interesting, short films of 6 to 10 minutes in duration, directed by and starring A-list talent, that could be viewed on the Web. In 2001, Fallon produced five films for BMW, using directors like John Frankenheimer (*Ronin*), Ang Lee (*Crouching Tiger, Hidden Dragon*), and Guy Ritchie (*Snatch*), and actors Clive Owen (*The Croupier*) and Madonna.

Each film revolved around a central character, the Driver (Clive Owen), who exhibited passion, integrity, skill, and a sense of adventure—all qualities sought by the brand and hopefully by the target audience. The media campaign mirrored the launch of a feature film.

The agency did all it could to build buzz. A guerrilla campaign spread word on Internet movie sites, followed by a poster campaign that resembled movie posters hung in hip, urban areas and placed in newspapers and in trade magazines like Hollywood Reporter and Variety. There were even postcards hyping the series placed in trendy club racks.'

Other innovative programs included sending the first two films on DVD to Hollywood influencers, key press people, and VIPs; a presence at the Cannes Film Festival; a radio DJ program among 59 stations in 20 metro markets; and a PR campaign that got mentions of the series on CNN, ABC World News Tonight and Access Hollywood, as well as in USA Today, Entertainment Weekly, and the New York Times.

Before long, everyone was whispering about these cool new films showcasing BMWs, and driving people to go to the Web site to view them on their own.

According to a proprietary study, people in the core, ages 25 to 44, luxury car buyer category exposed to the advertising showed a dramatic increase in opinions of BMW's performance and brand perceptions. Purchase "receptivity" and planned dealer visits in this core group increased as well,[6] The agency reported in 2002, "Despite no major product launches, overall sales are up 19 percent through September, and sales of the 3 Series jumped 37 percent during the four month period of the campaign vs. the same period a year ago."[7]

The work also won golds for Fallon at the Clio Awards and the Cannes advertising festival. Some judges objected to the campaign, saying that the agency was being rewarded for production values that cost about $15 million to create. Though neither the agency nor the client will release actual production costs, BMW's total media expenditures remained slightly under those of Mercedes-Benz and about half those of Lexus. With annual levels of $10 to $20 million, the agency said that it was able to get higher response numbers than either Mercedes or Lexus in key measures.[8] Sales for the period tracked slightly better than Mercedes and almost double those of Lexus.[9]

In some ways, this is the brave new world creatives have long wished for. Now there's a chance for their ideas to be played out not only in ads and T-shirts and toys, but in all forms of visual entertainment. However, the decade is going to represent a tough transition.

In a way, we're moving back to the kind of challenges embraced by Mary Wells when she opened her own agency in 1966. Instead of coming up with just an ad campaign, she persuaded Braniff chairman (and later her husband) Harding Lawrence to paint his planes seven different colors, hired restaurant designer Alexander Girard to decorate the interiors, and engaged Emilio Pucci to redesign crew uniforms.

Besides thinking about creating original content, the postmodern creative department is going to have to adopt a media-neutral stance—as will the whole agency—and occasionally come up with big, impactful, nonadvertising ideas. Media-neutral planning, writes Mark Earls, executive group planning director in a recent issue of the British trade publication, *Campaign*, "is about big ideas, not taglines or TV scripts. It's about profound and transformative ideas; ideas that stop and engage our audiences; ideas that shape and drive a company, a brand, a product or a service."[10]

Many people think this is going to be a stretch for agencies—and especially for today's TV- and print-oriented creative departments. "Ad agencies are set up to make ads (look at the factory processes which were copied from '40s Detroit)," writes Earls. "They talk the 'big idea' talk and then show you a TV reel. . . . The thinkers—both creative and planners—are trapped within these processes and follow the concerns of their jailers. Rarely do they venture out in the sunlight and dare to dream big and profound thoughts."

WHO GETS INVITED TO THE PARTY?

The goal of becoming media-neutral and capable of developing new thinking reaches down into agency hiring practices. Besides attracting people from other disciplines—be it architecture or Greek classics or theater production—agencies are going to have to experiment with developing a new kind of culture inside the creative department. For example, at Carmichael Lynch in Minneapolis, chief creative officer Jack Supple says he looks for someone who has "a kind of twinkle in the eye and a hair-up-the-ass spirit that's different than the rank and file."

After that, he's looking for people who are hungry and will work long hours with minimal supervision. "We're looking for someone who adds something, who will add spark and flair for our culture," says Supple. "In their hearts, they have passion for what they do, advertising or not. We want people who are passionate about something outside this place as well as inside the agency. Are you a standup comedian, or do you go out and build boats? I don't care if you play the tuba at night, as long as you do something outside this agency."

In addition, Carmichael Lynch holds a series of Marketing, Intelligence and New Discoveries (MIND) seminars featuring such diverse speakers as an action figure artist, an archaeologist, and an FBI profiler. "Creativity is eclectic and it needs to be fed," says Supple.

Supple tries to organize things so that teams have primary accounts while also working on different accounts, which keeps everyone fresh. "When I started here, I had a creative director. When he walked into your office with a job, you didn't know what it was going to be—which was kind of exciting," says Supple. "Then we went to a group system and the diet got too steady." Recently, the agency did away with the group system and reorganized along traditional department lines.

Today Supple and his creatives work on two floors of the agency's Minneapolis headquarters. He said he keeps his "creative people in proximity," so they can bounce ideas off each other, because a lot of the power is generated "when one creative person sees something great going on from another—it's infectious." They keep in touch with other elements of the agency on a day-to-day basis, but they "live" with their fellow creatives.

The agency makes a point of hanging onto its people. There are few layoffs. Occasionally, top people are persuaded by money or new challenges to leave for another shop. Usually, it's what Supple calls "the spawning run to the sea," when young people reach a midlife crisis and feel they have to get out of the Midwest and try one of the Coasts. "Usually they come back as soon as they have their first kid," he says.

With such job security, one of the problems the agency faces with older employees is occasional staleness. "Everybody goes through a period needing to be reset," Supple says. Some agencies give people a sabbatical to help them work through this period. At Carmichael

Lynch, they do that, too, but Supple likes to put them on a new piece of business. As he says, "Sending people off to study at a university in Italy is a good idea. But we have work to do tomorrow. Day to day, it's sort of a matter of 'Pick up the shovel, because there's work to do.' At least here you know that if you do great work it's not just for testing. You will actually get your work produced."

The problem for Carmichael Lynch and other agencies in the United States will come when they want to break the model. Creatives like to live apart and prefer the two-person team for ideation. They are not going to be repurposed for work in the brave new world of nonadvertising ideas without a fight.

DO CREATIVES HAVE A RIGHT TO THEIR NEUROSES?

When all is said and done, agencies must come to grips with the fact that—for good or ill—the creative department is still the engine of the modern advertising agency. Unlike account service, no one is suggesting that it be eliminated. In the end, agencies are going to have to raise the bar for creatives. They must either deliver big, broad ideas for clients or collaborate with people who do.

To Lee Clow, the future will belong to creatives who can win the trust of clients, a trust based on agencies enlarging their own definition of creativity and expanding the mission of the creative department.

"If they really let us in, we'll be able to help them think better about their brand and marketing strategy," he says. "Because I want us to be regarded as thought leaders and business leaders. We're not just selling them a TV commercial. We should be involved in [every aspect of marketing], like we are with Steve Jobs and Apple. Let's talk about opening stores. What should we do on the Web? How do we manage the media? All those pieces leading clients and brands are the business we're in. So the intellectual dimension of our company has been getting better and better to go with our creativity. I don't think we're done. I think it's critical that our relationship is not based on our last ad, but based on the intellectual contribution we make to the clients in marketing and communications."

LEADERSHIP LESSONS FOR THE MEDIA-NEUTRAL CREATIVE DEPARTMENT

✔ In addition to great copywriters and art directors experienced in producing strong TV and print ads, do you have a few utility infielders who can create compelling content so entertaining people choose to watch it?

✔ Is your whole department focused on producing great ideas instead of just great executions?

✔ Are you ready to organize solutions that include no advertising applications at all?

✔ Is the ideation process open to everyone? Is it media-neutral? Have you allowed everyone to come to you with silly ideas on the chance one of them will dramatically change the brand?

✔ Is your creative planning-based? Do your top creatives trust the research being shown them and know how to "read around it."

✔ Have you fostered a culture that rewards success but does not punish failure?

✔ How successful have you been including and championing ideas from the margins—from promotions and PR and media—even if they cut into the standard media budget?

✔ What has agency management done to ensure that profitability is as likely to come from a powerful idea that does *not* use measured media as one that uses traditional media?

✔ What have you done to slow the cooking time for ideas and speed up delivery times?

✔ Are agency managers ready to embrace nonadvertising ideas, and do they know how to reap revenue and profits from it comparable to the kind of profits earned from advertising solutions?

✔ Do you have access to all the information and tools necessary to do your job?

✔ Are you giving senior staff an opportunity to recharge their batteries from time to time?

✔ Do you encourage people to have interests they are passionate about outside the agency?

✔ Do you return from pitches you have won or lost and give everyone in the creative department a chance to hear the pitch?

CHAPTER 4

Media Department: Can It Replace Creative as the Primary Source for Brand-Building Ideas?

To catch fish you must determine what they are eating. Then you can simulate the natural prey with an artificial fly that appears to be real food and behaves as though it is alive.

Tom Meade
Essential Fly Fishing[1]

The most exciting new category at Clio and other major shows is something called "innovative media." Although it is difficult to define, innovative media is changing the way brands are introduced into the cultural bloodstream.

Here is just a sampling of innovative media winners at Clio in the past two years:

- To sensitize people to the ease of getting guns, a South African antigun group built a vending machine that appeared to dispense handguns. (*Agency:* The Jupiter Drawing Room. *Client:* South African Gun Alliance.)
- To dramatize the threat from toxic waste being dumped in its sewers, the Auckland Regional Council painted sea creatures on storm drains, with the line, "Poison the Sea. Poison Me." (*Agency:* Saatchi & Saatchi New Zealand.)
- To demonstrate the strength of Samsonite luggage, a suitcase was allowed to move on a rail in a steel frame atop taxis so that the suitcase slammed against the frame every time the taxi came to a stop. (*Agency:* TBWA/Singapore.)
- A convex mirror was built into a poster for the *Economist* with the line, "Know what's round the corner," to help pedestrians coming out of a tunnel see whether they were going to run into traffic. (*Agency:* Abbott Mead Vickers/BBDO, London.)

These applications hardly seem like a threat to the brand-building potential of the world's leading established media channels. But actually they are. Though few people may have noticed any of these award winners when they first appeared, their effect grew through word-of-mouth and extensive press coverage. Print and TV commercials can give you reach—but they seldom have the same impact as stories in "free" media. Of course, these stunts were produced in most cases for less than a hundredth of the cost of a single TV commercial.

As San Francisco's Jeff Goodby says, "The time for TV and radio and print commercials, while still the best thing to do in many instances, may be limited. I'm not sure how long the 30-second television commercial is going to be a relevant way of advertising. In fact, one of the reasons there's a bit of malaise in this business right now is that people are confused not about the creative work, but about media. They're going, 'Yeah I just did a great 60-second TV commercial, and I don't feel it had the same impact as the one I did 10 years ago.'

"In those days, if we did something ballsy, people were talking about it all over the place the next day. I guess we're starting to feel the creep of the TiVo machines. The kind of attention people give television nowadays is different. There are just too many buttons to press and too many other things going on in your life to think that a single commercial is going to change the way people view a brand."

That's a startling statement from a great creative leader who made his name with TV commercials ("got milk?" Nike, E*Trade, Budweiser, and Polaroid). He's just saying what is on many people's minds. The mojo seems to be draining out of paid media. The networks' market share has fallen in the past 20 years to the 50 percent level—but that's not the only problem. If you're willing to tolerate a short delay, you can employ technologies like TiVo that will erase commercials from your programming altogether.

"TiVo creep" and "attention competition" have two discernible effects.[2] First, agencies are being forced to come up with new forms of innovative media to generate buzz. Second, the model for planning media has changed from simply matching a matrix of media choices against a demographic model of the consumer to asking how relevant each segment of preferred media is to the consumer and where the best contact points are for reaching that consumer.

DOES YOUR AGENCY HAVE A SENSE OF PLAY?

The appetite for innovative ideas is everywhere. In Amsterdam, a hot, playful agency, KesselsKramer, highlighted Nike's sponsorship of a coming soccer tournament by pasting a filter in the shape of the Nike swoosh over the orange light in all the spotlights. For its work for Oxfam, the British-based food charity that wanted to call attention to unfair dumping by rich countries, KesselsKramer developed a campaign called "Make Trade Fair." Because Oxfam had no money for media, the agency persuaded shipping companies to let them stencil the logo on their freight containers. Suddenly, thousands of containers stacked on docks, floating on the sea, and being trucked to delivery points were proclaiming "Make Trade Fair," all at virtually no cost to the client.

In New Zealand, to promote the nation's lottery, a butler with a silver tea service was stationed at bus stops. In New Zealand, Saatchi & Saatchi Auckland stationed a smashed car outside movie theaters screening *Godzilla*. Absolut vodka built an ice hotel in Sweden to give its marketing a new dimension. UNICEF stenciled a message on leaves to dramatize the plight of war-weary Afghan children facing a bitter winter. In Australia, Vodafone's agency hired two men to streak at a rugby match with the name of the client painted on their backs.

The interesting thing about such placements is, first, they are so unusual that they make viewers want to talk about them the next day. TV commercials—even during the Super Bowl—have trouble doing that today. Second, they are so relevant, at least to the product, that they probably have greater impact than an ad. But what's really going on here is that we're moving from being intrigued with the Absolut bottle to becoming fascinated with the way advertising is moving back into our lives. If you see a billboard saying "Make Trade Fair," you might ignore it or wonder briefly what it means and pass on. If you see the same words stenciled in huge block letters on a dozen stacked containers on the back of a freighter, you might more easily grasp the irony that this is a commercial message against dumping on a freighter carrying products from rich countries to poor ones. Here is a case where KesselsKramer was able to leverage free media for Oxfam and catch attention at the same time.

MOVING FROM INNOVATION TO
CONTENT CREATION

So-called guerrilla or viral marketing is not that new, but it's growing in importance and frequency. If people see a celebrity they admire wearing a Rolex watch in an ad, they know it's an ad and therefore discount the message to some extent. But when they see the same celebrity wearing the same watch in a James Bond movie, they feel compelled to buy it.[3] That's why BMW introduced its Z sports car with a placement in *Goldeneye*. Those involved in the launch say it was effective.

The goal of these new marketing models is to come up with an event or stunt so audacious that it gets the marketplace talking about the brand. They capitalize on simple word of mouth, one of the most powerful forms of marketing communication ever invented. Awareness skyrockets when such promotions are picked up by the news media. Something that begins in real life and then is disseminated by news stories can reach still further through ads excerpting quotes from news reports about the real-life promotion.

Agencies are being pressed to pull such rabbits out of their hats every day, as consumers increasingly regard advertising as a nuisance— and are developing filters to tune it out. New ways of introducing or promoting brands have to be invented. One method—which is really just the return to the form of advertising that built radio and television programming 50 years ago—goes under the general rubric of *creative content*.

Creative content refers to the building of various forms of entertainment for the express purpose of promoting a brand. Goodby's TV campaign featuring the two lizards, Louie and Frankie, might become a cartoon series about the lizards or might be built into a sitcom about two bachelors trying to make it with chicks, using the same actors, stage names, voices, and attitudes of the lizards. Even if Budweiser didn't advertise on the program, the company would benefit, because the voices and characters of Louie and Frankie are inextricably woven into the Budweiser brand. Under current arrangements, Budweiser holds the rights to the characters and would be paid a license fee for the usage.

Keith Reinhard, the chairman of DDB Worldwide, recalls how in the 1950s *Fibber McGee & Molly* was a hit radio show every week. "You always knew Harlow Wilcox, the announcer, was going to drop in and show Molly how to polish her furniture with Johnson's wax," says Reinhard. "The product was part of the plot. If 'Whassup!' [DDB's famous campaign for Budweiser] had been introduced in 2010, it would have been *The Whassup Show,* not a commercial."

MTV, after all, is nothing more than a sales channel for the music industry, and placement is "free." The only cost is the making of the videos. When the videos are well done and the music is right, a great video can kick-start a new album or artist. Fans even tune in for the debut of the video for a new album.

Among other examples, The Michelin Guides were started as a promotion for Michelin tires, whose aim was merely to encourage people to think of Michelin when traveling or looking for a great restaurant. The guides are so well done and the restaurant and hotel rating system so respected, they have become a brand and profit center unto themselves.

If agencies put on their thinking caps, they may be able to come up with even bigger ideas. The Hummer car, after all, is quickly becoming the ultimate symbol of testosterone. The brand would be a cinch as the basis for a television show (sitcom or reality-based) aimed at young men interested in adventure or extreme sports. Hallmark is about connecting with people emotionally. Instead of the long-running *Hallmark Hall of Fame,* the brand might do better to start a Web site to help lost kids find their way back to their parents, or something with a love-based theme, or a show called *The Hallmark Moment,* a reality-based drama about reuniting children separated at birth from siblings and parents.

Jeff Goodby warns that there are limits, however, to the commercialization of content: "I think ultimately people will feel nettled if their entertainment is full of product placement, with people holding labels turned to the camera. It's going to start looking like Jim Carrey in *The Truman Show.* I think people want some part of their lives to be free of advertising. I remember when Channel One started and they offered everyone in school an Apple computer if the kids would watch an Apple commercial before the day started. Parents hated that idea. Think of what they were getting in return for just watching one commercial—a whole school of computers—and parents still didn't like it."

In the new era, however, there may be more acceptance of brand-related content as long as it is truly entertaining or helpful. I'm a passionate fly fisherman. I'm not going to mind a show about great fishing spots sponsored by Orvis, or even featuring Orvis products, as long as it's interesting and the information is true and is not just a 30-minute Orvis infomercial.

"Everybody presumes that advertising is bad," says Goodby. "No one ever considered the radical notion that we could make advertising that is so good, people would seek it out and want to watch it. I think that's the way things are going to go." He can see the time when kids will learn that a new X-Box commercial is going to break at a certain time of day—and will go to the Web site to view it.

Web sites could archive short films and content from other media and replay them in exchange for showing people a short commercial—the same trade-off, after all, that is the basis of broadcast television. "I believe that in the future this is going to be so important, you may find an advertiser is willing to fund the cost of producing a TV show in return for the chance to show it on their Web site," says Goodby. "For instance, you might go to IBM to see the next installment of *The West Wing* or view the *Sopranos* on the Cadillac site.

"Sure, there would have to be some kind of interruption, but at least we would maintain the wall between entertainment and advertising. People are going to want that wall. I predict we'll go through a period where the mixing of ads and content happens and then you'll see a backlash."

THE OTHER REVOLUTION: GETTING BEYOND DEMOGRAPHICS

For the past 40 years or more, advertisers have defined their audiences by age groups and told their ad agencies to go find them. About 20 years ago, we saw a minor refinement in this approach: the move to psychographics. Audiences could be defined by mind-set or lifestyle, not just by age and gender. As psychographics grew in power, agencies developed digital models that sliced and diced the demographic and psychographic models for more precision. At one time, proprietary research systems were even boasting that if you told them the names of two or three magazines a consumer read, maybe with a zip code thrown in, they could tell you what products that consumer would buy—of course, always qualified by a small margin of error.

Recently, media researchers discovered that they were losing audiences with this methodology. That was puzzling. True, you can define many Honda buyers through a combination of demographics and psychographics. But apparently, even with the right audience, the message wasn't getting through—not because it wasn't crafted in a sufficiently creative manner, but because it appeared in a medium or at a time when the consumer was advertising-resistant.

Suddenly, advertisers started to become aware of the importance of the context in which their message appeared and demanded more precise measurements to find out whether the message made contact with the consumer. Certainly, the dawning of the Internet heightened the growing realization of the fragility of marketing communication—because although Internet sites could prove that users had seen a message and even clicked on it, research showed there was no awareness. The user had filtered out the message or backed out of the encounter before the download was complete, because the user was so turned off by all Internet advertising that he or she wasn't interested in considering a new application.

This is a truly revolutionary development. It has forced media planners and buyers to become much more sophisticated about how they position their communications—not only on the Web but in traditional media. As a result, we are starting to see the development of a *matrix*, or *cascading*, message strategy, whereby you try to get the intended consumer to see your message on a highway billboard at about the same time he or she is hearing the same brand message on the car radio.

As Nick Brien, president of U.S. Business Development for the giant Starcom MediaVest Group, explains, "We are now looking for contact innovation. The metrics of brand creation need to be more than mere media metrics. When you think of the big brands—Coke,

McDonalds, Philips—they don't need more brand exposure. The customer knows them. They need to engage the customer with messages that are relevant and contemporary and presented in an interesting way. Our whole strategy has got to change. Brand engagement is what it's all about.

"And to do that it all goes back to insight. *Insight! Insight! Insight!* The stronger the understanding between the brand and the consumer you want to engage, the better the chance that those insights into the consumer will shape the communications strategy going forward. Communications is content *and* contact. It's not just a game of metrics any more."

Brien thinks advertising needs a new discipline—what he calls *channel planning* and others call *contact planning*. Brien defines channel planning as a fusion between account planning, where the planner seeks to understand behavioral characteristics of the consumer, and traditional media planning, which plots the demographics and psychographics of target consumers against a media map.

A channel planner is able to think beyond just buying the so-called right shows for a targeted audience of 18- to 24-year-olds (e.g., for Levi's "engineered to fit" jeans). Just buying time on a hip program, like MTV's *The Osbourne Show,* might not be the best way to project cool. It might be cooler to identify the jeans in a certain market with a brand or an event. Even better might be some kind of promotion that would appear first—with the ads to come later. In other words, for the ads to be welcome, they have to come in contact with consumers at the right time of their lives, through the right channel, or they will be rejected or ignored as being inappropriate regardless of the message they carry.

Part of the challenge is not only finding the relevant media but the right time of day. Kids today multitask. There is a certain time of night when they can be expected to be doing their homework—all the while Instant-Messaging their friends and listening to rock music. There are other times when they take in a little TV while calling a friend on the phone or scanning a magazine. This in itself makes it difficult to send them any commercial messages. But they also have filters that immediately sense an ad and tune it out.

Meanwhile, they may have a "cool index," which tunes out dumb ideas—based on the channel over which a message is transmitted rather than on the message itself. If Levi's doesn't want to fall into the "not your father's Oldsmobile" trap—in other words, to be regarded as the badge of the baby boomers (read *parents*), then it has to be careful not to play its ads on shows that kids see *as directed at their parents*—even if the kids enjoy watching them, too! Net-net: Beware of guilt by association.

"We're no longer focused only on behavioral aspects of media versus account planning, which is more attitudinal," says Brien. "It's got to be a combination of both in order for our contact strategy to really engage the consumer. We need a new mind-set in the traditional media company that is no longer focused on conventional exposure. You need to understand both attitude *and* behavior, and find out where they intersect."

DEVELOPING A CONSUMER-CENTRIC MEDIA PLAN

Most people who have pondered how to get agencies to assume a more media-neutral posture call for a revolutionary change in the way media plans are developed. The change has already started, as some agencies seek to recast media professionals as "channel planners" or "contact planners." This involves teaching planners not only to consider cross-media applications but big, nonmeasured media ideas.

"In my view, media-neutral planning is probably the biggest issue of all [facing the advertising industry], being a culmination of all those issues that came before," writes Tina Kaye, former DDB London planning director and, more recently, former marketing director of Conran Design. "It is not just about the big idea that can span different media. It is, in fact, fundamental to the way in which a brand does and should touch consumers' lives. It is the planning of those brand touchpoints without bias toward or against any particular mediums or channels."[4]

"There is a new breed of cross-media planner," writes Don Cowley, managing partner of London's DLCF Integrated, "but many media agency people seem happier within a channel rather than across channels. Few agency teams include experts in contract publishing, product placement, or event management, but a good strategist will know the consumer effect of those kind of media."[5]

"Media planners have to evolve in the agency of the future," says Rosemarie Ryan, chief strategic planner for Kirshenbaum Bond & Partners. "The job is not just to work out what is the right program for this ad, as an answer to the simple question of, 'Are we getting enough GRPs [gross rating points]?' It's to understand how we can connect the consumer to the communication and really understand who is the target audience beyond demographics. Who the people are, where do they live, what do they like to do, and how do we find new interesting ways of reaching them—this is a much bigger job."

She says that her agency has stopped calling the workup a media plan but has retitled it a Brand Exposure Plan. The Brand Exposure Plan, she says, "predicts wherever the target comes into contact with the brand. It defines the contact point. And that helps tell us what we can do or say to solve a particular brand problem."

The old planner, of course, would ask what shows people watch. The new kind of planner, according to Ryan, needs to be a media strategist. She cites a hypothetical assignment from client Target stores to launch a campaign to remind mothers of its toy offerings at Christmas. "I would expect the new kind of planner to know where kids and mothers hang out together," she says, "To know what they want for Christmas. And being consistent with Target, to recommend something opportunistic and not expected."

One key to the new media planning, as Ryan points out, is involving planners from the start. In the United Kingdom, where Ryan trained before coming to the United States, media people are held in higher regard by creatives than in this country. As she says, "They had a seat at the table from the beginning of the conversation. It was creative media ideas that got the creative people excited."

WHERE DO WE FIND THESE NEW PLANNERS, AND HOW DO WE GROW THEIR SKILLS?

To recruit the new kind of planner, you have to be careful not to limit your search to people with measured media experience. "We need smart, creative account planning strategists," says Brien. "People who can coordinate and execute across various platforms. I'm looking for someone who is in love with brands and in love with consumers and who is very focused on brand relationships and attitudinal direction a brand has taken, rather than just looking at a consumer group from a behavioral point of view. These two worlds aren't connected right now. But I want one person who can do both of these things."

Within an advertising agency—or an unbundled media agency— other skills will be needed to sell through this kind of thinking. Just as media people need to understand account planning, account planners are going to have become more media wise. "There needs to be an understanding of the general complexity of brand marketing in the modern media company," says Brien. "Too many traditional media practitioners are worried about placing the right ad in the right media with the right target audience in the most cost-efficient way. That's important, but it's not enough any more to ensure that the content is going to have the impact the client demands. There's no cost efficiency when there's no relevance or effectiveness."

Finally, strategic media planners are going to come at a premium. Some may pull down salaries as high as creative directors. Agency managers and CFOs are going to have to be creative and learn how to sell their services to a client. Such planners can work on many accounts over the period of a year, so their services can be costed across many budgets. But they must be more than just a new business ploy. When they make a difference in the client's business, then clients shouldn't mind paying extra for their contributions.

BIG IDEAS THAT GO WAY BEYOND MEDIA
PLACEMENT AS WE KNOW IT

Say you were given the Hummer account, and the first thing the client wanted was a new ad campaign. Like all clients, Hummer will have a budget limited, if not by imagination, then by some balance sheet metrics. Maybe ads aren't the first thing the agency should suggest.

"Sometimes it's better to pull back and say, 'Wait a minute, I want to talk to the new consumer first. When we're ready, we'll do an ad.

But first let's get our heads around the idea that should be bigger than a traditional ad,' " says Brien. "Perhaps it's a multicultural event or a PR strategy or branded content on HBO or MTV. I would take that idea to the studios out in Hollywood straightaway and say, 'What can you do with a Hummer?'

"If you can't make it into a sitcom, it might be a game show. Or it might be something with a band. It might be with Eminem'or with whatever is the hottest thing going on at the moment. Do you pair up with the agency in the Hummer family? Sure. Otherwise, you would be presiding over a horrendous political maelstrom. But I'm no longer intimidated about telling the client to let us take the lead. The modern client has little patience with politics and demands a business-building idea regardless of where it came from."

Brien has experience selling his ideas to Americans. After running Leo Burnett/London for five years and building it into that competitive market's agency of the year, he moved across the pond in 2001 to the Starcom MediaVest Group, where in his first year he helped win that global media-buying giant $250 million in new business. "The reason this kind of contact management strategy is going to be the wave of the future is that the client is not thinking about who can make my next TV ad," says Brien. "The client is thinking about the next business-transforming idea, driving real value creation. If it's a script for a new TV show centered on the Hummer, fine, go with it. Then it's up to us to find a screenwriter and hire a director. Agencies aren't quite ready to do that—but they will be."

The bottom line: *If agencies don't prepare their media teams for this brave, new world, someone else will.*

Brien and others find agencies today ill-equipped to fulfill this mandate. After surviving the rigors of reengineering, few agency managers are interested in introducing yet another planning discipline. "The agency and even big media companies like ours, are typically looking at media consumption—not what I call 'contact management,' " says Brien. "We are no longer just looking at the relationship of the brand and consumer and how that impacts traditional media. Those two things have got to be married together in a new way. That's why at SMG we're actively hiring account planners to develop this new discipline."

Brien thinks agency leaders have to redesign their agencies from top to bottom. "I would start fresh," he says over a summer lunch at Smith & Wollensky's, a favorite Second City watering hole of the advertising crowd overlooking the Chicago River. "To start with, I would decree an end to the ridiculous separation of media and creative. Full stop. But I would also declare traditional full service dead. If you have true full service—twenty-first-century full service—offering both analog and digital holistic thinking, then full service is without doubt the best structure for the most efficient delivery of brand power. But how many agencies can make that claim? Most agencies are still stuck in a mass broadcast [mind-set] of marketing. They present all of their diversified skills in silos. Integration is far harder than diversification.

"Media consciousness, media thinking, media power, fast-changing consumer behavior, interaction with the brand—creative agencies have a very limited understanding of these concepts. And of the continuing power of technology in marketing. Unless they are intellectually curious and excited by these transformations, they won't get it. As I've said to many creatives, 'Get with the reality of what's happening. You can be the best blacksmith ever known to man. When the motorcar comes along, it's over.' You have to reinvent yourself with the whole idea of modern transport or get out of the way for people who do."

WILL MEDIA BUYING BE AN INTEGRAL PART OF THE AGENCY OF THE FUTURE?

The jury's still out on this critical question. Agencies are victims of their own business models. If clients won't retain their so-called agency of record to do their buying, then it's only natural for that agency to begin to dismantle its media department—or limit it to a planning function.

One veteran, Matt Bryant, who built Media Buying Services (MBS), now the backbone of Carat's U.S. operation, into one of America's first unbundled media shops, believes many agencies will retain some buying function after they realize how critical creative media buying and planning capabilities are to winning and keeping new business.

"My theory is that the whole cycle is beginning again," says Bryant. "It's a question of the poacher becoming the gamekeeper. People who are giving up on their media departments are moving into very dangerous ground. Give up this territory to the large unbundled services, and, in effect, you're giving up part of your knowledge base."

Bryant makes the point that ideas for interesting media solutions don't just come from planners—they come from sellers of media, too. The sharing of such ideas grows naturally from both sides of the negotiation process and the strong relationships that are formed between buyer and seller.

"I always bet on the person with relationships," says Bryant. "Ideas can come from the drawing board or the give-and-take of normal business. Particularly if you have a small budget, like an Ikea, that needs to bob and weave. I would bet that Ikea wants people to tell it about opportunities to stretch its budget. So you go to your pal at the network and say, 'How can you help me here with Ikea?' You get the creative juices going. And bingo, suddenly you have a sponsorship opportunity nobody ever knew existed. That's what a company like Ikea tends to be looking for—the value-added and big ideas. You can't get that by calling someone on the phone for the first time."

As with agencies pitching creative accounts, Bryant starts every media pitch by trying to get closer to the client. "I get on the bus and try to see the client—if not the guy in charge, then his local retailers and distributors. You want information about where his customers come from, the demographic, what's the media budget, what makes his cash register ring, and what are the relationships they already have that can be leveraged with local media. There's no substitute for talking to people who deal with those customers every day.

"Then I go out and find local media people who have dealt with the client. The big guys are used to buying *Seinfeld* and outdoor in bulk. I want to find the opportunities at the street level and know what grabs the attention of consumers. You're not just buying morning radio from seven to nine o'clock. You're buying a certain station and its quirky talk jocks. You have to know the station manager to know where are the opportunities to push your way in. I used to get so close to some stations, they would call me and say, 'Something canceled and we decided to give you block of free time.' And I would be incredibly appreciative. That was the depth of our relationship. They knew what we wanted and they took a chance that we would approve the addition without even calling me. It's terrific when it gets to that stage."

A SURPRISING FUTURE?

If Nick Brien and people in his camp are right, then there are some big battles ahead for the soul of the modern advertising agency. This chapter may have made it sound like the new media department threatens only the creative department. But it goes much deeper than that. If media departments are redesigned and empowered to become brand strategists, they could take on some of the functions of account service.

"It's all really just a question about how should the client spend his money," says Brien. "That's the Holy Grail. Everyone's asking how ambitious strategic media people are these days. Well, let me be plain about this: I want to do more than just be at the table when they determine the architecture for the brand strategy. I want to be the architect. The brand deserves the most impartial, the most strategic, the most creative architect for its communications. And I cannot be there unless I have a very profound marketing mind-set as well as a media mind-set. I need both."

As Brien sees it, media and creative might one day stand on equal ground: "The day may come when the client feels more comfortable turning over his budget to the media director than to the account manager. Someone has to be responsible for defining and designing all brand communications and contact. Why not a contact strategist? As the lines between contact and content start to blur, as I believe they are, then there may be more important questions to be settled than what is the size of the logo and what's the best headline, and who is going to carry the client's bags to the next sales meeting.

"The critical questions may be which contact, what contact, how contact—all the province of the contact strategist. We're talking PR, we're talking events, design, advertising, sales promotion, direct mail, sports marketing—but the point is that advertising is now only one element."

As Nick Brien watches his colleagues from various Chicago agencies mingle on the steakhouse's power porch in the midday sun and contemplates what he sees as an opportunity for media agencies to broaden their mission, a devilish look comes over his face. "The day the client gives the account to the contact strategist," he says, "well, I would call that World War III, wouldn't you?"

LEADERSHIP LESSONS FOR CHANGING FROM STRAIGHT MEDIA PLANNING TO STRATEGIC CHANNEL PLANNING

✔ Go beyond demographics and psychographics in defining the target and explaining how it consumes media.

✔ Be aware that the channel over which your ad passes may be more important than the message.

✔ Just because a viewer or user sees your ad doesn't mean the message has been digested. Failure to absorb an ad's message may have more to do with channel issues than a creative message.

✔ Respecting the way your target audience reacts to media may be as important as the way your target regards your brand.

✔ Within your agency, seek out a new kind of media planner—one whose skills are more closely aligned to account planning than to media buying and who can analyze these kinds of issues.

✔ Train your planners to evaluate media, not just on the reach and the frequency needed to get an impression, but on the impact and the relevance with the target.

✔ Learn to distinguish between tactics and strategy. A channel planning strategy is a two-year plan. A tactical media plan is an executional buying or placement plan of a few months' duration.

✔ Think twice before giving up your media-buying capabilities—but evaluate buying media by what kind of relationships you can build and leverage to develop value-added ideas and opportunities rather than as a simple revenue center.

✔ Start treating your media department as a critical creative resource, perhaps even more important to the development of new brand-building ideas than the creative department.

✔ Change the way you sell media buying and planning capabilities to your clients. If they're commodities, someone else is probably going to be able to deliver them faster and at a better price.

✔ Sensitize your staff to the importance of innovative media, and start entering your agency's best work in this field in award shows. This will raise your standards and make your people more aware of how this new field is developing.

✔ Designing an effective brand strategy requires time, money, and insight. To excel, agencies are going to have to invest in hiring and grooming brilliant media strategists and then give them the same kind of resources that traditionally have gone to creatives. That may be a terrifying thought for the cash-strapped agency CEO, but a dynamic strategic media strategy could be the deciding factor in winning new business for your agency.

CHAPTER 5

The Internet and the Agency

American fishermen have pursued trout across our continent's northern streams and lakes for decades. Now there exists a third dramatic cold-water fishery that has expanded the trout's ranges deep into the South. Just as tackle and techniques differ with lake and stream fishing, so does this new fishery call for specific methods if you wish to meet with reasonable success.

David Whitlock
Sports Afield, April 1971[1]

There are two great implications for advertising on the Internet: First it offers access to almost all consumers all the time. Second, it threatens eventually to erode the value of almost every other form of media.

Fortunately, as with all new technologies, new media enters our lives in stages. Contrary to popular belief, the real potential of the Internet has so far barely been understood.

As with the arrival of every new medium—be it radio, TV, cable, or digital—there's a time of fascination and intense interest. This is followed by a period of some disillusionment. In the early days of Internet hype, absurd claims were made, encouraging owners of the great broadcasting, newspaper, and magazine franchises to sink vast sums into Internet applications—with no hope of recouping any costs except through advertising.

This proved an illusory dream. Advertisers were at first intrigued with the Internet's ability to document what is known in the analog world as *impressions*. Sites that were fortunate enough to get users to register could offer demos that were precisely defined—and could then tell advertisers the time of day and the amount of time users spent visiting a site and its ads. Suddenly, advertisers had the opportunity to display their logo to or push a communication at consumers with much more efficiency than other media. But the appeal of the numbers being delivered by these sites was diminished with the growing realization that their communications had little or no impact.

Before long, it was discovered that even if a user clicked on a banner, it was unlikely that any meaningful communication took place. Either the technology was so leaky that the message took too long to load and the user backed out of the encounter, or the message was so lame it had no effect. Banners were animated; sound, light, and action was added; and even a promotional offer or game was introduced—anything to get the user to tarry awhile and experience the brand. But click-through rates continued to fall, and research showed little of what was really going on. Too often, even if a user was transported to the advertiser's home site or to some kind of selling ground, the communication was so irrelevant or the technology so frustrating that users lost interest. A few sites even tried to turn such encounters into sales. Rates for these "conversions" were even dimmer.

By the end of the 1990s, investors in Internet technology realized they had been cruelly deluded about the value of what they were buying, and the dot-com bubble burst. Except for eBay, Amazon, Expedia, and a few other high-visibility sites, the retail potential of the Internet dissipated, and advertisers began asking hard questions about whether they were getting any real return on their advertising investment.

The Internet was introduced in the United States in 1980. Within a few years it was connecting millions of people around the globe to sites of every imaginable description. I had hosted a number of Internet marketing conferences in the 1990s, including launching first the Adweek Forum at Internet World and, then with founder Skip Brickley, Ad-Tech. These conferences quickly became a must-attend form of professional education. There simply was no better way to keep up with developments of marketing in the digital space.

But it was all predicated on interaction between advertisers and consumers, which was never consummated. The fact is that Don Peppers and Martha Rogers were right: the Web *is* the first mass medium of one-to-one communication. Showing or touching your customer with a communication is not the same as having a satisfying, complete interaction. Worse, if the experience is disappointing, it can actually degrade a brand's value.

Users were enticed by notices in analog media to visit the sites of their favorite brands—be they retail brands like Nike or Levi's or business-to-business brands like IBM or Hewlett-Packard—for information about new products or help with a problem. The experience was often a disappointment. In some cases, the sites were so complex that they were difficult to navigate, or queries might never be answered for lack of sufficient customer relationship personnel. If a great brand like IBM disappoints you when you visit its headquarters on the Web, you have to ask whether its promise of e-business customer service holds water in the analog world.

Exceptions were sites like Lands' End, Honda, Dell Computers, Amazon, and some hotel chains that immediately sensed the potential of the Web and made huge investments in their sites to ensure a transparent, intuitive, and successful customer experience. Today, for instance, it is not unusual to look at a Lands' End catalog, call an 800 number, and begin placing an order, only to be directed by the telemarketer to the Lands' End Web site to see different views of a product. The relationship between catalog, telemarketing, and digital marketing is virtually seamless, with no pressure to use one over the other. Online, Lands' End experimented in the field of custom-made jeans and chino pants. The program, created by Archetype Solutions, allowed the user to input contour information and receive a custom-made pair of pants four to six weeks later. The effort surpassed all expectations, driving 40 percent of jeans and chino orders on the site within a year.

Furthermore, some brands have created a seamless continuity among their different retail outposts. For example, Barnes & Noble bookstores, Pottery Barn home furnishings, and Eddie Bauer outdoor apparel, among others, all encourage people to buy from their Web sites, but honor returns of those purchases at their retail stores.

DON'T DESPAIR, ONCE WE GET THE HANG OF IT, THINGS WILL IMPROVE

As long as usage is climbing, the marketing potential of the Internet remains strong. Instead of worrying about falling click-through rates or the diminishing power of banner ads, advertisers should be pressing their agencies for more creative ways of communicating with online consumers. If traffic on Sunset Boulevard doubled in a period of two to three years, would anyone think of ignoring the potential for billboards on that famous Hollywood thoroughfare? Somehow, there has to be a way to make the Internet advertising experience more valuable. Instead of denigrating the medium, advertisers should be hammering their agencies to come up with more effective kinds of communication.

"We're moving into a world where digital or what I call 'information protocol technology' will sooner or later flavor all media or marketing," says Rishad Tobaccowala, executive vice president of the Starcom MediaVest Group and one of the pioneers of Web marketing. "Consumers use it regardless of what the Nasdaq is or what companies come and go, primarily because it allows them to do things they couldn't do before."

Tobaccowala, who has more than a decade of experience with digital marketing, first at Leo Burnett, then at its digital subsidiary Giant Step, now at Starcom, believes that besides the magic of e-mail, the Internet empowers consumers with information and knowledge that previously did not exist in other places. "It is the first medium to give consumers all the qualities we've been looking for. It delivers the infamous four Cs: control, choice, convenience, and communication."

Usage continues to climb. Consumers are now using the Internet more than an hour a day, compared with four hours for television. Not only are businesses forcing their employees to buy air tickets and reserve rental cars on the Internet, people are learning how to shop for cars and even houses online. Kids can burn their own CDs from Internet music sites. Not only can you book a room at one of the three hotels on the tony Ile de Saint Louis in Paris, you can actually view the room you may be staying in.

"A lot of younger people consider it more important than television," says Toboccowala. "And of particular interest is the fact that they use it simultaneously with television and other formats. And the same technologies that make the Internet happen are slowly coming into the television set, through set-top boxes and personal video recorders like TiVo, so gradually we're starting to see the convergence people have been waiting for [over the past] decade."

WITH INTERNET USAGE RATES CLIMBING, WHAT'S HOLDING IT BACK?

On the flip side, Tobaccowala notes, it's still hard for advertisers to learn how to market over the Internet. Previously, they had viewed media as a *push* format: On TV, in magazines, and on billboards, advertisers pushed their messages at consumers. Suddenly, consumers are deciding which messages to select. It's a *pull* format. Before you can talk to consumers, you must entice them to spend time on your site. According to Tobaccowala, "From a consumer perspective, I control my programming and [with TiVo] I can edit out commercials. And so the underlying basic belief is that in the future, the impact of the Internet on television is going to grow over time. But marketers are going to have to learn how to approach this from the consumer's perspective."

Tobaccowala insists there is no mystery about how to accomplish this. He posits that consumers are drawn to things they are passionate about. Tap into their passion, and you can be assured of their attention. As in all media, he says, "It's nothing more than relevance or ensuring that your message is placed in the right context. But interestingly, the relevance on the Internet can be much deeper than in other media.

"For instance, I'm interested in children, but not just anything about children. I'm interested in how to feed children. You tend not to find television programs [that are narrow enough] to answer these kinds of interests. But now you have sites which are that narrow. Over time, the economics are such on the Internet that it may be easier to get the right programming which is in tune with your passion or your interests. So the idea is what we call Passion Group Marketing™."

The new technology, then, would allow users to program either their computers or their computer-enabled televisions to search the Internet for programming or new content aligned with their passions. It will just be a matter of coming home and reviewing what's been downloaded to your personal video recorder. Instead of the 100 or so channels now available on cable, the Internet will offer programming from literally millions of channels. The home information and entertainment console will be able to download and save that programming so it may be searched and viewed at a time convenient to the consumer.

"The personal video recorder is a combination of a hard drive and some software," Tobaccowala says. "It has the capacity to save up to 100 hours of programming. That is my channel. I program the content for myself. I'm not talking about 40 years from now but a world that is only four or five years away." The challenge for marketers is to stop thinking in large demographic segments and to start zeroing in on smaller clusters of consumers who are more desirable.

The trick, says Tobaccowala, is to program content appropriate to such clusters. "So, for instance, if we want to get young people, instead of looking for programming that has a high proportion of young people, we will, say, look for adjacencies with particular programs that have a very high degree of passion for this cluster. It's like what we call *upside-down marketing*. Instead of starting with what the broadcasters have available, go back to what is particularly applicable to the consumer and the brand.

"If you're selling cars, you have to ask: Where do people go when they are particularly interested in cars? And what do car owners also have multiple passions for? Do car owners have a great deal of passion for travel? Then perhaps I can reach the cluster from a travel site. Passion Group Marketing™ doesn't replace demographic or other types of marketing, it enhances them."

TV WAS A "PUSH" MEDIUM: ON THE WEB, USERS WILL "CHOOSE" ADS

"What has made the Internet so hard to market to is that the consumers are in control of their computers," says Tobaccowala. "Now they're going to be in control of their television. So you're going to need to crack the code. We're not talking about product placement, really. But delivering a value. That value might be information. It might be entertainment that extends the value of a site. It might be that an advertiser will underwrite programming. But whatever you do, in the future, you will have to find other ways to understand your consumers and new ways to provide them with something special.

"To summarize, technology is going to change the way marketing is done, because marketing increasingly is going to be user-controlled. And it is going to basically be an area where we're going to have to learn what consumers want and what they're passionate about. And how that relates to how much they use your product."

This insight should provide encouragement to the publishers of magazines and owners of cable television channels with definable niche audiences. If they can deliver these audiences in the analog world, then it's not much of a leap for them to establish parallel sites in the digital world. *Vogue* is a brand that represents the best in women's fashion, whatever the medium. *Money* magazine knows how to talk to middle- and upper-middle-class people about protecting their investments and retirement funds. In the case of trade magazines, the niche is even narrower and the control of content even stronger. Magazines have been successful in getting advertisers to pay for their overhead. When they transition to the Web, circulation income tends to disappear. And advertisers complain that the digital model cannot give them adjacency to content with the same power and graphic resolution as the analog, hard copy world.

So the business model will have to evolve. Having aggregated an audience, a media site is going to have to be more creative in how it integrates the advertising experience into the consumer's visit.

First of all, Tobaccowala thinks advertising is getting a bad rap. "If you go to *Bride's* magazine or *Fly Fishing* magazine and ask someone, 'Would you think more or less about this magazine if it had no advertising?' people would say they love the ads. The reason is that those ads are very relevant to their passion. They are saying that they're passionate about getting married or fishing. Therefore, anything that is associated with fly-fishing or marriage they accept."

Magazines or TV channels operating on the Web first of all need to do more to be sure their advertisers add value to the site and don't detract from it. They may have to take more care in what kind of advertising they solicit or create discounted rates for ads they deem to be informational and relevant. That way they can ensure that the user's experience will be positive, whether working through the site for information or advertising.

TIME TO BLUR THE LINES BETWEEN
CHURCH AND STATE

Next, there has to be more experimentation in letting advertisers become involved with content—but with more control than is exercised by space salespeople and publishers in the analog world. "Let's assume one thing about the Hummer is that it allows you to cross riverbeds," says Tobaccowala. "So then I would say, 'Look, can you do stories about the problems fly fishermen have accessing sites?' If I'm going to do my own advertising, I'm going to talk about the way Hummers cross riverbeds [being] great for fly-fishing, or sponsor a story about riverbed crossing and ensure that a Hummer will be featured in it.

"So it becomes in everyone's interest to make it less than a Hummer message, but we get across the point that a Hummer helps you pursue your passion. Hummer may put an ad adjacent to a story about remote fishing—and the ad starts off with how the Hummer helps me solve my problem.

"Does that mean we have to create more narrowly targeted ads with higher production costs? Perhaps. I will go to a site, but we may want to buy content and real estate relevant to that content simultaneously. Say, for instance, kids like Corn Pops. Kellogg's may want a Corn Pops message or a Corn Pops game. So we will go to Yahoo! and instead of asking them to put up a Corn Pops banner, we will use my media dollars and say we know Yahooligans is very popular with young people.

"We know that people come out of school and have to do their homework between 3 and 6 P.M. They often use the Yahooligan as their resource. So during that time, we would like to own the Yahooligan home page. But instead of advertising, why don't we pay you to create a very interesting game, which is animated on the page. And people come there to play that game, and if they want even more information, they click and they go to my site, where they can have even more fun with Corn Pops. So, in effect, what have we done— we've not only bought media, we've bought creative. We've basically hired Yahoo's engineers to tell us how this might be done."

Tobaccowala thinks this will result in more revenue, not less, for media sites. Instead of paying $100,000 for four pages in a magazine, an advertiser might pay $100,000 for a certain number of impressions and editorial space, plus $20,000 worth of programming to assure that its relevant messages are properly communicated. Advertisers, whether in the analog or digital world, will be buying space for their ads and assurance that the content next to it is relevant to their target. This is scary territory to some editors and publishers who have built their bond with readers and viewers on a promise of editorial independence shielded from pressures of advertisers.

But Tobaccowala believes advertisers will demand only relevance, not control over the actual words and pictures. "You're buying the right to say, 'I want to be sure the content is about this if I'm going to be next to it,' which is what you have now in many magazines," he says. "Call it whatever it is—you want to put product in the context of the editorial in a way that makes sense. So if the Hummer doesn't make sense for fly-fishing, say so. If it does, I'll pay for it."

The advantage of this model is that even if the cost per thousand increases in the Web model, advertisers will be spending less on advertising that's wasted, because the Web has a superior capability for precision targeting of narrowly focused markets.

"Let's suppose today a client has $100 to spend on advertising," says Tobaccowala. "Today you've almost spent that for high-reach media for one or two ads. Tomorrow you might spend $20 [in nondigital media] and $40 for digital media and $40 for messaging. So you're giving up something. You're giving up all those exposures against people who basically did not matter in exchange for more who do. The problem is that however narrowly you define the target, you're going to miss somebody. But in this model you're spending less on advertising that's wasted and more on advertising that's very targeted. You've got to realize neither by itself makes sense anymore."

WHAT DOES THE TRANSITION TO DIGITAL MEAN FOR AGENCIES?

The agency's role in this evolution is to guide and direct it. Clients will continue to rely on media planners and creatives to advise them on how best to allocate their advertising expenditures. Again, if agencies choose not to become experts in dealing with interactive media, then clients will look for others who are. Reliance on managing brands may move from traditional agencies to innovative or large media planning and buying conglomerates. It's the agencies' game to lose.

Fallon demonstrated a comfort with the Web by devising the BMW Films campaign. David Lubars, the agency's creative director, who made his reputation by creating and directing great print and TV ads for 20 years, had no qualms about selling the client on a Web-based campaign that depended largely on feature-film writers, actors, and directors.

The current practice of not tasking ad agency creative departments to design digital solutions is off-base. If the new era requires agencies to be media-neutral, it doesn't ask them to be media-stupid. Agencies should bring interactive creative departments in-house. There should be art directors and writers as confident of working up digital applications as analog ones. Perhaps they will have to turn to digital production houses—just as they do for the postproduction specialties in print and TV. But they need to have more digital intellectual capital within their four walls in order to program the Web intelligently.

This will become clear when we finally achieve the long-awaited convergence between the computer and the TV screen, which Tobaccowala believes is only four or five years away. Actually, it already exists in many households in the United States. These homes are abandoning dial-up for the convenience and speed of cable modems and DSL. With a more robust pipeline, it will be possible to deliver 30 frames a second video with no download delay to the computer screen. If it's on the computer, some enabling technology can move it to a digital format on the TV screen.

When that door finally and fully opens, then the same skill sets that made powerful TV campaigns will be valuable on the Web. The only thing missing will be the inclination of the consumer to watch these campaigns. Because the Web is by its nature a pull medium, users will have more control over what they watch. Jeff Goodby may be right that users could be persuaded to barter away their right to tune out commercials in return for access to premium content like

Sopranos. It's also possible that they could be trained to seek out commercials for brands they find engaging and/or relevant to their passions. A fly fisherman might choose to see the latest Orvis rods in action. A car driver may want to find out more about Honda SUVs. Similarly, an agency could create a whole film about the Budweiser lizards or the Taco Bell chihuahua. The only difference is that whereas 30 seconds on prime-time TV can sell for $250,000 to $2 million, 30 minutes on your own Web site is virtually free. The only substantial cost is for production—and whatever lure you have to use to draw people to your Web site.

Concerts can be sponsored on the Web in the same way they are today on TV. Web sites could offer users a chance to download music in return for listening or watching an ad. Users might even be willing to give up information about themselves in the form of online registration in exchange for a chance to view or download premium content.

SOMEONE'S GOT TO PLAY THE ROLE OF CONDUCTOR

Ad agencies are the natural orchestrators of this kind of experience. They already employ planners who through research or instinct know when such communications are appropriate. Their media people should be able to plan such placements and negotiate their appearance. Their creative people should be skilled at designing them and fitting them into the brand's overall media mix. However, agencies have cut back on digital resources in recent years due to the recession. It remains to be seen whether they will want to get back into the game. To do so, they are going to have to find ways to drive revenue from digital applications while waiting for broadband to roll out to homes and offices.

"So we're not saying the world is coming to an end," says Tobaccowala, "but what we're talking about is somewhat unfathomable in today's climate, and there's no way to get to the next level unless you put your oar in the water today. The reason is basically that we're no longer talking about the Internet, but about the future of marketing and television. Just bring one of these technologies into your home and watch what happens with young people. Something like the personal video recorder is very easy to program if you know how to use a remote control. Once you've mastered it, you become addicted to it. Then you start to say, 'Okay, I've changed, so obviously the people I market to have changed, too.'

"Now, if you're ready to accept that we will have access to programming on the Web that we will want to record, then you're going to want to figure out what the new thing is. Organizationally, we may not be set up for this frontier. Agencies may require a different kind of talent than what you find in the typical creative department. I don't think someone who is spending 95 percent of their time on 30-second commercials is going to have the time and inclination, in effect, to want to spend time destroying the 30-second commercial. Creatives won't be the ones to destroy it, of course. Consumers are going to destroy it. So agencies are going to require different skill sets if they want to exploit this new appetite for content."

Tobaccowala believes, as I do, that in this new frontier clients may be expected to gravitate away from ad agencies and toward robust media companies, providing they're staffed with people of vision. "I've always believed that if the future is about marketing, it's much less about advertising and media," says Tobaccowala. "In the old days there was a triangle consisting of the client, the agency, and the medium. What tended to happen was that the agency would buy the medium and develop the content for the medium.

"But in the new world there are going to be all kinds of applications. So you will have things being done by the advertising agency, the promotion agency, the PR agency, and the media company. Now clients are going to say, 'Who becomes my lead horse?' But the client may not be interested in buying all these services from the same company. If that's true, the client may want to turn to their media company to be the linchpin of integration. The media company, after all, already decides how the dollars are to be spent. Media people are already more central to the strategy. They can talk to a lot of different people about the kind of content that's necessary for the media they buy.

"It doesn't mean the ad agency disappears, it's just that the media company is the more natural integrator. A lot of media today is buying with scale, having lots of technology so you can do the targeting and optimize spending. An ad agency is no longer a scale business. It used to be, when the media company was bundled into the agency, but that's no longer the case. So if you take media out of the equation, then an ad agency lives or dies simply on the quality of its ideas and its creative."

In this model, there may be one media company orchestrating the marketing and directing for several creative agencies—one that specializes in print, another for TV, and another for digital. Media companies are today heavily into technology for measuring effectiveness and ROI, but they lack the sophisticated planning skills required. "Media separated from creative long ago because of a lack of respect by creative people for media choices. But the new media director needs to understand better and have more respect for the creative process," says Tobaccowala.

"The central media company becomes very important in this [new model] because they have the scale to have the relationships with all these people; they have the scale to invest in all the technology to do all the measurement," says Tobaccowala. "What they don't have fully developed is a basic understanding of marketing and the idea-driven talent which may be needed. A few media people have been trained in some of these areas, but not enough. So you may come to a world where, instead of skill sets organizing around client service in a creative agency, they'll likely gravitate to planning strategists at a media company. But then media companies need to gear up for this scenario. Whoever is going to orchestrate the marketing needs to be very open to ideas and thoroughly understand the contact communication process."

This might require a new kind of media director—Tobaccowala calls this person the *messaging director*—one who is as likely to be drawn from the world of account planning as from media planning and buying. Media people by their nature today are too involved in metrics and finite measurement. Creative directors know only too well that sometimes good ideas often have to be bought on instinct. If media people want to take on a broader mission, they are going to have to get comfortable with the daring and contrarian approaches of bold, creative thinking.

"In the end," acknowledges Tobaccowala, "We may have to attract higher-level, brighter people moving into the media space."

LEADERSHIP LESSONS FOR UTILIZING THE INTERNET

✔ Agencies need to increase their skills in digital marketing at a time when advertising expenditures on the Internet are decreasing.

✔ Digital skills should be integrated throughout the agency—but they are most important in the creative and media planning departments, which must be relied on to come up with new kinds of Internet-based promotions for clients.

✔ Internet marketing messages must be so entertaining or interesting that consumers will seek them out.

✔ The secret is relevant, passion-based marketing that seeks to deliver marketing messages in the right context and at a time when consumers are naturally seeking help from brands in solving problems or satisfying needs.

✔ Some consumers may be willing to barter away their ability to tune out messages in exchange for access to premium content or entertainment.

✔ Agencies should review their own business model to ensure that they can derive as much profit from an Internet application as from any other kind of media placement. This new world may put more of a premium on programming and production than on media space, but, either way, the cost to the client may be about the same.

✔ Agencies that resist this evolution will find their role as integrators of media ceded to the more advanced media agencies.

✔ Media agencies that wish to exploit this opportunity will have to recruit a new kind of media director, one who understands the creative process and can make judgments in choosing and integrating the right mix of creative producers.

CHAPTER 6

Prioritizing Strategic Planning

[The seasoned fisherman] also "feels" the pulse of the river. The weather, the water level, temperature, and water clarity are good indicators, as are insect activity and a score of other factors that filter through a mind that has analyzed these situations time and time again. Between success and disappointment lie the flukes, the unexplained and even the humorous aspects of sports afield.

Roger Menard
My Side of the River[1]

The advertising world's fascination with strategic planning has been more than a decade in the making. For a time, I helped organize conferences on the subject. Over several years in the mid-1990s, Stuart Sanders and I presented a dozen or more experts on both sides of the aisle, including Martin Sorrell, chairman of WPP Group, owner of Ogilvy and J. Walter Thompson, who complained that agencies were giving away the "crown jewels" of marketing; Sam Hill, a leading marketing strategist and author (*Sixty Trends in Sixty Minutes*, John Wiley & Sons, 2002) who had worked at Booz Allen and then signed up for a stint as head of strategic planning at D'Arcy; and Andrew Parsons, who headed the consumer and global marketing practice at McKinsey and delighted in winning strategic marketing assignments from big clients.

Adam Morgan, former head of account planning at Chiat/Day, spoke at one of these conferences about his ideas for helping "challenger brands," a subject he later developed into the business bestseller, *Eating the Big Fish: How Challenger Brands Can Compete Against Brand Leaders* (John Wiley & Sons, 1999). Morgan appeared on our programs at a time when there was much confusion between account planning and strategic planning, two very different disciplines, and he was one of the few planners who could do both.

The reason for this interest is partly financial. Beginning in the late 1980s, when clients abandoned 15 percent media commissions as a basis for paying their agencies, agency revenues plummeted. Suddenly they were having to justify every hour for every person on an account. In an effort to cut costs, agencies began laying off or repurposing senior account executives who had the training and experience to serve as strategic planners, and they cut back or eliminated the in-house research departments that had supported them. Agencies lost their ability to deliver this kind of intellectual capital in a disciplined manner. At the same time, clients experiencing the downturn of the 1989–1990 recession found themselves in greater need of strategic counsel. The void was being filled by outsiders, and agencies were having to execute marketing strategies developed by third parties.

Today in the typical agency, senior account executives with good instincts and brand knowledge still offer valuable insights to help a brand grow. But they lack the research and fresh data to support their judgments.

Moreover, few agencies have organized such executives into a separately branded brain trust that could compete with the likes of Booz Allen and McKinsey for a serious assignment. While the opinions of agency people may be solicited by clients, agency executives are not properly compensated for their judgments (i.e., beyond their standard hourly rate), nor is their advice on major issues taken seriously.

"Clients think of agencies as a tool, not really as an analytic force," says Sam Hill, who is now president of Helios Consulting, a strategic marketing firm headquartered in Evanston, Illinois, and formerly vice chairman and global director of strategy at D'Arcy.

According to Hill, if agencies are serious about competing with the major consultancies, they're going to have to be prepared to make an investment in people, tools, and research. He cites the $20 million-plus that Young & Rubicam reportedly spent on creating its Brand Asset Valuator as a smart first step in creating unique, proprietary intellectual capital that would attract major clients. "It was genuine research, not brain candy, and it definitely got the attention of clients at the highest levels," says Hill.

In addition, he thinks agencies need to find different people to act as strategic planners rather than trying to send in the account team. "You need a different set of guys. You can't show up with the account manager and expect to be accepted as a guru. The client deals with these people all the time and knows they don't really have the same level of skills and experience of a marketing strategist. I remember attending a seminar by one of the big consultancies for Royal Caribbean. An agency account person told the client, 'This wasn't such a big deal. We could have done that.' And the client told him flatly: 'No. You couldn't!' "

Also, agencies need to find top-level people who know the client's business well enough to offer marketing insights—instead of attending sessions run by their subordinates and just showing the flag. Hill cites a D'Arcy briefing for Rick Wagoner, chairman of General Motors, to which D'Arcy brought 30 people.

"Top guys at the agency have to get their hands dirty and really understand the client's business. You've got to be able to sit down eye-to-eye with a John Pepper [former chairman of Procter & Gamble] or a Rick Wagoner and engage them on their problems," says Hill. "No CEO wants to talk to 30 people about his most intimate problems. But one-on-one, that's how strategic assignments get sold."

SOME AGENCIES ARE READY TO WALK THIS TIGHTROPE

DDB Worldwide is an exception. DDB has set up a management consultant unit, called Matrix, with offices in Chicago and London. Currently, its biggest client is Dell computers, which has used the unit on a regular basis to understand pricing issues and chart advertising expenditures through a discipline called *econometrics*.

Another DDB unit, Demand Consulting, based in Chicago, is more classically organized along the lines of a strategic marketing consultancy. Demand Consulting advises clients on new product development and turns the insights of account planning and strategic planning into action plans. Both units operate outside the normal DDB advertising relationship and therefore require separate compensation. Clients know they are getting a separate service because ideas are presented to them in a formal manner by people different from advertising teams working on their account.

"The creative solution clients are likely to get from Demand and Matrix is far different than what they're likely to get from Booz Allen or McKinsey," says Jim Crimmins, chief strategic officer at DDB and the senior executive to which both Demand Consulting and Matrix report. "Our understanding of the consumer is far greater than these outside firms and the actionability of the results is greater—because our people have access to the advertising people who work on the brand on a day-to-day basis."

But Crimmins acknowledges that his units are more limited in their perspective. They don't have the resources of a McKinsey to go upstream and examine the research, development, and manufacturing processes that impact a brand—or downstream of the advertising to study its distribution and retail channels. Matrix is focused on telling a client the implications of its media spend. If it raises its spend to $90 million, would ROI increase, and by how much? Similarly, it can measure what would happen if the brand changed its pricing structure or threw all its budget into print instead of television.

Demand Consulting is more focused on strategy. It was hired by Tyson to help position not only chicken, but through recent acquisitions, beef and pork products as well. Conducting some very innovative research, Demand was able to isolate what causes consumers, at breakfast, lunch, and dinner, to choose one meat over another. Demand Consulting then helped Tyson extend the brand into other meal occasions by understanding how consumers choose meat options.

"Booz Allen may be better at the grand scheme and the supply side," says Crimmins. "They can tell you how to streamline manufacturing or distribution. But the understanding of the consumer is far greater from us."

In another case, Demand showed Morton Salt several new product categories it could enter simply by licensing the Morton name and sharing its understanding of distribution and consumers with licensees. "I don't want to create the impression that this [Demand] is a huge, thriving business," says Crimmins. "But we're beginning to earn money from nonadvertising clients and clients outside our normal advertising contract.

"Occasionally, we're asked to work for someone—fee or no fee. But it's less trouble than I anticipated. Clients see that what we provide is really above and beyond the normal business of advertising. It would be very difficult to persuade them this is a separate service if we had the exact same people they see every day. They would then say, 'I'm paying for these people already, why should I pay more?'

"But when you bring in a new set of experts who do this and nothing but this [kind of strategic work], experts they don't see on a day-to-day basis, then they understand why they have to pay a little more for that type of service, and frankly, they appreciate it more."

Crimmins emphasizes that "there is business to be won" in this sector if ad agencies learn how to leverage their special competencies. "Many of the resources that Demand Consulting uses are resources that can be used by DDB. We have access to a variety of tremendous databases. For instance, we have a Life Style study we've been doing for the past 27 years, involving 3,500 people, asking them 1,000 different questions about attitudes, purchases, media, and so forth. We have a Brand Capital study in which we look at 2,500 brands across 23 countries around the world. That is quite useful for advertising development, but also can be used for brand consulting. These are all extra tools a start-up in this area wouldn't have."

The other point he makes is that as big agencies get bigger, the pool of available clients grows smaller, making it increasingly hard for agencies to increase revenues by increasing clients. Agencies will have no choice: They must develop their expertise in brand building and try to move into strategic planning. "Agencies" he says, "use planning to win and serve clients not to make money directly and separately. But the same skills can be applied to other marketing issues, and that has the potential to generate new revenue."

Meanwhile, agencies would do well to study Matrix's franchise and ask themselves if that's an area they want to try to develop. The demand for economists schooled in the science of *econometrics* (the science and art of translating economic data to a metric that can be tracked and forecast) is growing. But it's difficult to find trained practitioners. "People who can do this well and turn it into recommendations for client action are very hard to find," says Crimmins. "The hardest part is gathering data and cleaning it. Clients have mountains of data. Making sure it makes sense before using it for modeling is the trick. But once you can tell a client not only the effect of what his ad spend is today, but what it would be tomorrow, and you prove out the ROI, it becomes a tremendous tool in helping a client make choices."

In the midsize agency group, Fallon has jumped into the fray with its Fallon Brand Consulting unit in Minneapolis. The unit has grown in two short years to 12 employees in Minneapolis, where it has set up shop in offices six blocks from the company's headquarters.

Managing director Bruce Tait says the agency wanted to make the Fallon name synonymous with "really smart brand strategy" as well as strong creative services. The unit has so far been successful in winning clients primarily outside the Fallon roster—including assignments from Gulfstream Aerospace; Ask Jeeves, the Web search engine; Speedo bathing suits and goggles; DKNY apparel; and a biomedical device company, Guidant.

"We've grown like gangbusters," Tait says proudly, noting that in its second year, revenues increased 89 percent. He credited part of the unit's success in not trying to sell its services to the agency's advertising clients. "Inevitably, you run up against the [territory] of account service and account planning, and the internal political structure of the agency forces you out, or you get into conflict issues. That's why we have separate offices and a fire wall between us and the agency. We want to be able to take on clients in categories where they [Fallon advertising] already have clients."

Tait, who originally was trained as an account planner and worked for BBDO in Canada before joining Fallon in 1996 as group account planning director, says the move to brand consulting was a relatively easy one for him—even though the two disciplines are very different from one another.

"Account planning I think necessarily takes place inside an advertising agency," he said. "There, you are working to bring consumer insights to the table to drive communication solutions. We think of brand consulting more broadly. We're not only looking at a communications brief but positioning the company from every touchpoint—from packaging to the way the company hires people."

On the other hand, he believes because of the unit's links to the advertising world and his people's creative orientation, the company can draw on skills and a point of view not native to the larger marketing consultancies. At companies like Booz Allen and

McKinsey, he says, "brand strategy has become the province of a very analytical process that leads to a very dry conclusion." Instead, he believes that agency-based brand units such as Fallon's, by using mostly retooled account planners and being closer to the advertising process, are able "to bring more original thinking and creativity to the positioning of ideas."

YOU DON'T HAVE TO BE A GIANT TO HANG OUT A SHINGLE

Tait makes it all sound relatively easy, but to enter this field successfully, agencies must seriously rethink their structure and business model. Keith Reinhard, worldwide chairman of DDB, says it's partly a problem of perception: "Marketing consultants and brand consultants see themselves as magnificent architects. And once they've completed their plans, we, the agencies, get to bid on the 'building' they've designed."

Reinhard goes on, "We can't continue that way. We have to expand vertically into the consulting space at the same time we expand horizontally into other marketing services so we can be perceived by clients as both brand architects and brand builders."

Part of the secret to success is packaging. "It's not just a matter of hanging out a consulting shingle," Reinhard says. "We have to present people who are as knowledgeable about a client's business as a consultant would be and who are honestly good at coming up with business-building ideas. Clients turn to marketing consultants, and pay them a ton of money because they present themselves not as someone trying to sell advertising, but as business gurus. Clients pay these consultants for their experience and for their processes. We have to learn how to do this.

"The consultant comes in and says he's going to interview people around the world for, say, $150,000 and then analyze the responses, and, for another $150,000, he will give you a summary presentation on where your brand stands. We have the ability to do that, and we have the tools and methodology to do what the consultant does, especially since much of the consultant's presentation is boilerplate. But once again, it's a matter of perception.

"It's like, if you're in an operating room and there's a guy standing over you whose reputation is not as a surgeon, but as a dentist, and he's trying to tell you, 'I can perform this operation better than the surgeon,' you're going to say, 'Get out of here, you're a dentist!'

"Even though we might be able to construct a brand foundation better than a consultant, the client is still too often saying, 'Get out of here, you're an ad guy. We'll call you when we need some ads.' This is what we get for our years of saying, 'All we want to do is make ads.' If we hope to get paid for our thinking, like consultants do, we need to present ourselves differently, as more than just ad guys. We're making some progress by selling consulting services through our sub-branded units."

Reinhard admits that transforming agencies into brand architects and brand builders will require a total rethink of account management. "If you think in terms of the traditional account manager role, that will be obsolete," he says. "If we're going to charge for both strategic thinking and multichannel execution, we'll have to have a new kind of person—someone who can think about the client's business at a higher level and someone who knows every aspect of brand building. We've talked to business schools about the need for this new kind of person, but so far there hasn't been too much progress. The Medill school [at Northwestern University], for example, has a real commitment to what they call Integrated Marketing Communications, but they are not media-agnostic, which is a must. They come at everything from a database and direct marketing point of view and miss the importance of the big picture."

As for management consulting, Reinhard is not interested in seeing DDB trying to compete with McKinsey to tell a client which factories to close. "We don't know anything about that. We should be focused on marketing consulting at the top level," says Reinhard. "Our competency is in telling a client how to go to market, how to build brands and manage a brand portfolio."

THAT OTHER KIND OF PLANNING

There is no Marketing Hall of Fame to celebrate all the new products that have grown out of an advertising executive's intuition. But there should be. After all, it takes insight to suggest that a hotel stay be individually tailored to a customer's personal preferences (Wyndham by Request, from Kirshenbaum Bond) or that teenage girls would prefer a cosmetic line already prepackaged in a plastic carrying case (Caboodles, from DDB). All you have to do is be reasonably insightful, be steeped in a brand's DNA, and be constantly looking at consumers to determine where they are going next.

This brings us to the evolving role of planners. Account planning is a discipline developed in Britain in the late 1970s and early 1980s. Most credit Stanley Pollitt of Boase Massimi Pollitt as its founder. He saw the planner as a trained researcher who would gather all the data possible on consumers and, based on that data, have an equal say with that of the account executive in the forming of the agency's brief and with that of the creative director in determining the creative strategy. Gradually, the top planners, like Jon Steel, who trained at BMP and later took over planning at Goodby, Silverstein & Partners, grew suspicious of the mounds of scientific data being collected by advertisers and began simply spending more time with consumers, observing their habits, how they used a company's products, and how they viewed the brand messages being pushed at them.

"Account planning was conceived as a way for agencies to treat the very affliction that ails so many American advertisers and agencies today, by creating and maintaining meaningful relationships with consumers," writes Steel. "The planner's role in the process of developing advertising [is] to use their input at every stage of the process to inform and sometimes even inspire creative ideas, and to guide and validate the resulting advertising campaigns. . . ."[2]

Today, a good planner can deftly chart the equities of various brands in a particular category, showing blank areas that are still "open" and therefore provide opportunities for brands to grow in new directions.

It doesn't take much to move from that kind of brand equity mapping to actually coming up with new products to fill certain voids. Often, consumers themselves, especially in focus groups and one-on-one encounters, will tell planners things they wish a brand would do. They may even reveal the actual new products they want or believe they need.

But such insights, again, tend to be easily uncovered and lightly presented. A smart client in the presence of a top planner like Jon Steel will carefully mark such insights and move them deliberately to product development for consideration and testing. It doesn't matter, after all, whether the idea for a product comes from within a company or the marketplace as long as it fits a real need. Starbucks, today a $3 billion company with a global chain of coffeehouses and branded coffee—available from the airborne galleys of United Airlines to the shelves of your local supermarket—was built on the simple pleasure enjoyed by founder Howard Shultz in a Milan coffee bar, sipping espresso, and on his belief that the experience could be transferred to a corner store almost anywhere in the United States.

Yet the account planner's work is still costed as an hourly adjunct to the modern agency's creative process. No agency—at least none that I am aware of—has yet thought to build a strategic marketing and consulting company around its account planning department and tried to sell its services separately from its advertising. Such insights should be, in the lingo of the venture capitalist, *scalable*. Equity mapping is a somewhat rote business growing out of interviews and data. But deciding how a brand should be repositioned and where its growth potential lies, or waking up a dying brand—such contributions are high-stakes businesses deserving of a premium. Successfully defining fresh ground for new products is an even more valuable art, worth far more in long-term returns than any mere ad campaign, however valuable.

The fact that no one has yet done it says more about the conservative nature of ad agency management than about the potential of account planning.

"You need a compensation structure built around the idea," says Steel, who has returned to London and is currently working at WPP, helping subsidiaries deal with planning issues. "I've worked with design and brand consultancies who are able to charge for work which agencies customarily give away in new business pitches. If agencies could figure out a way to charge for their ideas, which is really the most important work they do for a client, they would be in a much better state than they are right now." (See Appendix A for Martin Sorrell's landmark speech on this subject.)

FOR SOME AGENCIES, PLANNING IS ALREADY
THE CENTRAL FOCUS

Not everyone is trying to wring the last dime out of planning. Bob Schmetterer, chairman of Euro RSCG, has ordered his advertising network to come up with new product ideas on a regular basis for clients. He sees this as the next big thing agencies should be doing for clients. Besides energizing his network with his own internal Creative Business Ideas™, he's also established a Global Planning Council, headed by Marian Salzman. (The idea grew out of the Brand Futures Group run by Salzman and and partner Ira Matathia at Young & Rubicam.)

"I don't see this as a profit center, but hopefully it's an idea center," says Schmetterer. "We want to assemble the best planners we have, regardless of where they are in the world, and not only cross-fertilize each other, but . . . mobilize against specific client opportunities as they come up." He's not ready to challenge the current business model so as to make planning a separate charge, though he says that Euro RSCG planners occasionally draw an assignment from a nonadvertising client. "The business model that global agencies have is that we basically give away the strategic thinking and thought leadership in return for the revenues we get from creating advertising, direct marketing, interactive, and the other services," says Schmetterer. "On a rare occasion, we will change the model: We did a tremendous amount of work for Hallmark which led them to introduce Hallmark Flowers—and never produced advertising for them."[3]

In the end, both strategic planning and account planning work best when they are idea-focused. Jon Steel saw planners working only from within an agency structure, advising the creative department, because that was how they had been deployed in the agencies where he had worked. As he wrote, "Planners may have to work very hard to influence the way that the advertising turns out, carefully laying out a strategic foundation with the client, handing over tidbits of information to creative people when, in their judgment, that information will have the greatest impact, giving feedback on ideas, and hopefully adding some ideas of their own.[4]

Steel doesn't regard planners as being a prime source of new products, just new campaign ideas. But as DDB's Jim Crimmins points out, the job of planners today is not only to synthesize data, but to make data actionable. That can mean either through a new communications message that repositions an existing brand or through the creation of a brand extension or a wholly new product. Either way, planners are putting the brand on a better path—"growing the brand," in modern marketing parlance. The trick for agencies now is to reorganize their operations to be better able to harvest such ideas and drive that growth.

"We need to change our processes so that we work to have ideas that solve business problems," says Mark Earls of Ogilvy & Mather London. "This means more than just having super planners thinking super thoughts for others to color in. It means engaging one group of thinkers whom our industry has selected on the basis of their ability to solve problems—the creative department—in strategic discussions. . . . And we need to rethink how we get paid, not only because it makes this kind of thinking between different disciplines really difficult, but also because it doesn't put any value on the idea."[5]

LEADERSHIP LESSONS FOR EFFECTIVE STRATEGIC PLANNING

✔ Agencies can increase their competency in strategic planning by training senior account people in the discipline or recruiting new people who already possess the requisite skills.

✔ Agencies should consider retitling these executives as *brand planners* or *communications planners* to keep them from being confused with account managers or account planners.

✔ To be taken seriously, the planning function should be carried out by people in a separately branded unit capable of earning fees outside the advertising relationship.

✔ Strategic plans should be actionable—they should easily become the basis for new advertising campaigns or, in some cases, new products or product extensions.

✔ Strategic planning is a discipline totally separate from and broader than account planning, which is focused only on the consumer. However, account planning and other forms of research should provide the basis for such strategic insights.

✔ Strategic planners should have the ability to look at all kinds of issues extraneous to the advertising—price, availability, packaging, competitive product set, brand heritage, changing demographics—to determine a brand's viability.

✔ Agency-based strategic planners should be able to compete for assignments with independent marketing consultants—and the results of their studies should be presented to clients using a formal process similar to how independent marketing consultants package and present their conclusions.

✔ Management of a brand involves marketing and many other disciplines, including finance, research and development, manufacturing, and so on. Agencies entering this field have to decide how far upstream they are ready to go.

✔ If agencies cannot form their strategic planning efforts into a separate revenue center, then they should ask whether they even want to be in this business.

✔ Strategic planning has to be given the time and resources to do its job properly. If it's a process-light, idea-on-the-fly kind of business, clients can be expected to regard it accordingly.

✔ If clients see the same people who plan the strategy of their brand planning their advertising, they have every reason to ask why they have to pay extra for the former, when they are already paying for the latter.

PART 2

Management Lessons

CHAPTER 7

Growing Your Agency

Trout fishing during stormy weather can be a nasty business.
When the rain starts to drench your old fishing vest or the snow
pellets peck at your favorite hat, my advice is to get under
cover, build a big fire, and stay put until the storm blows over.
But there's one trouble with this bit of Spanish philosophy—
you don't get any trout.

Tom Henderson
Sports Afield, June 1954[1]

The phases of growth for a new agency can be charted with almost the same regularity as for that of a child. At birth, the agency is struggling to breathe and to find sustenance. It either wins those first new accounts or succumbs. With its first accounts, the principals will be buoyed by a sense of omnipotence. This is the feeling that Mary Wells evokes so well in her richly anecdotal account of the founding of New York agency Wells Rich Greene in 1966.

"Braniff gave Wells Rich Greene its first account and the big Braniff color program moved into high gear shortly after we opened our doors," writes Wells in her book, *A Big Life (in advertising)*.[2] "*Fortune* magazine photographed everybody at Wells Rich Greene sitting on the blue wing of a Braniff 707. I sat in a peacock chair. That Technicolor spread of Wells Rich Greene in *Fortune* says it all, Blessed Bunch. By the time Braniff's colorful planes got into service and were flying around America the country knew all about the airline and the planes and Emilio [Pucci's crew uniform designs] and Wells Rich Greene. Many of the businessmen who visited us in our first months said they wanted 'a Braniff,' meaning an idea so big it would become the talk of the time."

After birth, the typical agency then proceeds through a few years of early growth, where its mettle is constantly tested by fickle clients, the economy, and its regional market. If it's very lucky, it may then break into the national spotlight. From there, the further phases of growth are shaped by the size of its billings and the brilliance of its advertising. A few agencies go on to national prominence. Of those, one or two more (e.g., Fallon and Wieden + Kennedy) get a chance to move onto the international stage. From then on management becomes very complex, as leaders struggle with the difficulties of managing a brand across many cultures and countries—and multiple brands for global clients. At this stage, or even long before, most agency owners would rather sell to an international network than go it alone. Once in a network, they are suddenly faced with demands for quarterly earnings, conflict issues that prevent them from going after new accounts, and pressures from the parent company to shape their culture to the network's needs.

WHAT IS THE RIGHT MODEL FOR STARTING AN AGENCY?

The old saw is that all it takes to open an ad agency are two creatives and someone who can count. Fallon, one of the most successful American agencies of this century, was started by five happy-go-lucky souls in 1981. Pat Fallon was a director of marketing services at Martin/Williams, another Minneapolis agency that survives to this day. His creative partners, Tom McElligott and Nancy Rice, came from Bozell and Jacobs. Fred Senn was the ultimate account guy at Martin/Williams. Irv Fish, whose insouciance and trademark bow ties betray a shrewd financial brain, became business manager. He says his main qualification was that he was the only one who knew how to draft a business plan.

The five brought no accounts with them. As principled professionals, they had not attempted to poach any clients from their former agencies. They shared a passion for the business and, in the first few weeks, won an assignment from a local TV station, then an insurance company, which turned on the cash flow spigot.

Things haven't changed that much in the past three decades. Agencies are still started by several partners with an itch. Ideally, the partners combine both good business sense and sharp creative thinking. But there is no one correct formula for a start-up.

Tracy Wong, an art director, and his partner Pat Doody, both graduates of Goodby, Silverstein & Partners, started WONGDOODY in Seattle in 1993 on their own. "There's only two functions you need from the beginning," says Wong. "Someone to handle the making of the creative widgets and a businessperson to talk to clients and keep you on the straight and narrow. Everything else in the early days can be handled freelance."

One element needed from day one is sound financial management. Agencies, after all, are businesses. Pat Fallon could find new business; Fred Senn knew how to service it; Tom McElligott and Nancy Rice were gifted creatives. But someone had to go to the bank to extend the agency's credit lines, negotiate contracts with clients, and restrain the partners from hiring too many assistants. "I was the guy who told them when they could have a copier," says Irv Fish, recalling those early days. Today the agency has copiers and all the other accoutrements for the making of advertising in offices in Minneapolis, New York, London, São Paulo, and Singapore—and billings of almost $700 million. Fish has handed off financial management, but he still comes in to talk growth with the partners.

"From the very beginning we had a financial plan and we had budgets," says Fish. "I remember at one point we emptied our pockets, figuratively speaking, to see how much capital we had. Without paying ourselves, without getting any business, we knew we could go to nine months. If we didn't get anything by month 10, we knew the market would be screaming, 'Go away!' "

THE EXCITEMENT OF A START-UP

Starting an agency is heady stuff. As Lee Clow, longtime partner to the late Jay Chiat recalls, the early days are in many ways the most exciting. "When creatively passionate people get together to start a company, the energy and camaraderie is really pretty stimulating," says Clow. "The feeling is, 'We're going to change the world. We're going to do stuff hasn't been done before. We're going to aspire to be whoever our heroes are.' " In the beginning, says Clow, he and his partners looked to Bill Bernbach, Carl Ally, and Ralph Ammirati for inspiration. These were all creative luminaries 3,000 miles away in New York who were changing the face of Madison Avenue.

"There's that energy every morning to try doing something great and succeed as a business," says Clow. "The only thing that was going on the West Coast was the L.A. branch of Ayer and Foot, Cone & Belding [in San Francisco]. These were big agencies that you kind of wanted to do a 'David and Goliath' to. In the beginning, the energy is just incredible, and then as you continue to evolve and grow you try to maintain that sense of family and camaraderie and passion. As Jay said, the question ultimately is, 'How big can we get without getting bad?' "

EVERYONE REMEMBERS HOOKING
THEIR FIRST BIG ONE

Landing a big account can make all the difference. Irv Fish recalls about a year into Fallon's meteoric founding, the infant shop was invited to fly to Denver to pitch Baby Bell US West. "Somebody at Northwestern Bell had heard about us," says Fish. "So we were included in a huge agency search. We got on an airplane. A sort of life's lesson for us—because you have to remember, except for going to Milwaukee, we had never pitched outside Minneapolis.

"We ended up being one of three finalists. All presented on the same day [in front of] 18 people who had flown in to hear the contenders and make a vote. I think we came second. We made our presentation and went back to the hotel. In fact, to save money we all checked out of our rooms and went to Pat's room to wait. At four o'clock we got the call with the news we got the business. It was a transforming experience. From then on we knew we could pitch anywhere in the United States. Suddenly we could go to New York or Chicago and people would talk about us as 'the new guys.' It took us a long to figure out just how far we'd come."

That's the nature of the ad business. You can leap onto the world stage with little advance notice. Winning a big account can save your bacon, losing one can put you in the soup. *Adweek* and *Ad Age* might as well be called *Sporting News*. They have built their franchises on handicapping the players. Agency competition for new business is charted on a weekly basis, and then at the end of the year a "report card" with grades for new business wins and creativity is issued. No agency is known to have sued either publication yet over such ratings—though some chiefs have written letters to the editor complaining about their grades. Billings growth is accepted as the ultimate measure of success.

Besides winning new business, an infant agency should do what it can to leverage the fresh perspective the partners bring to the business. If McCann-Erickson and Grey knew what clients wanted all the time, there wouldn't be any crumbs for the start-ups to feed off of in the early years. But the truth is that even large accounts can be lost or taken for granted at the giant agencies. The passion and ideas generated at young, smaller shops sometimes more than makes up for their paucity of resources and experience.

In the early years, when agencies are relatively small, people communicate easily with each other and there is a willingness to work long hours and do things beyond their job description. Later, walls are erected and turf wars break out. Media people withdraw into their own department and creative people separate themselves from research and account service.

IS YOUR MONEY GOING TO GROW FASTER IN THE STOCK MARKET?

Why start an agency? For some, it's an itch that has to be scratched. For others, it's a combination of ambition and greed. Given the fact that such a great proportion of young agencies fail, it's wiser to look on it as a chancy learning experience rather than as a smart financial investment.

"When friends ask me if they should start an agency, I tell them, 'Sure, give it try,'" says Brian Hurley, a founding partner of Grant Scott & Hurley, one of several San Francisco–based Goodby spinoffs. "Even the frustrating parts can be fun at times. If six months from now we lose everything and all end up back at FCB or Goodby, it will be well worth it. It will have been five or six years working with smart people. We have control over what we work on."

Jean-Marie Dru partnered with Jean Claude Boulet, Marie Catherine Dupuy, and Jean-Pierre Petit to start BDDP in 1984 without any business. Dru and Boulet had been running the Young & Rubicam office in Paris, planning their escape from the comfort of a grand multinational for almost a year, when they made the decision to go out on their own. Out of loyalty to legendary Y&R chief Ed Ney, they had trained their successors and explained the succession to all of the agency's clients, so no accounts came with them at the time.

The goal, says Dru, was to create "a beautiful company. We wanted to create a very contemporary, innovative company that happened to do advertising, as opposed to an advertising agency which happened to be innovative. We were determined to start a group of companies the first year—so right away we were in direct marketing, public relations, and so on," he says. "From the beginning, we focused on the values of the company—especially integrity and innovation. Integrity was very important at that time because it was the beginning of the bad habits [the lack of transparency in media buying] and there was a lot in the French market we didn't want to copy."

The foursome had the good fortune to catch the attention of the trade press and a couple of clients. Within a few minutes of opening on January 4, the phone rang. It was Danone, the giant French food manufacturer, whose president, Francis Gautier, said, "Listen, I don't have any business to give you at this time. But you can consider BDDP an agency of record for Danone." Soon after that, the client sent them a small account. The agency began building its brands with strong creative services and within three years was looking for acquisitions outside France.

BDDP's early growth was also sparked by embracing a set of radical new principles designed to challenge the then-corrupt French way of paying for media. Dru says that attacking the way agencies received secret commissions, or kickbacks, from the sale of media in France was "a very big bet—very dangerous for us. We had people threatening to blackmail us all the time," he says. "The fact that we were so constrained on media buying [caused us to be] seen as people with a lot of integrity. Integrity was important in everything we did. Because, if we said we were honest about media, then clients expected us to tell the truth about their business and about ourselves." An agency that embraced a new, transparent way of charging for media was a shock to the advertising establishment in France. Fortunately, BDDP was also able to develop campaigns as great as their chutzpah, and they soon became the toast of France.

Similarly, Fallon McElligott Rice in the first days took out a full-page ad in the Minneapolis *Star Tribune*, which today still hangs in the agency's lobby. The ad served as a little-veiled attack on the rest of the advertising agency business. The headline read: A NEW ADVERTISING AGENCY FOR COMPANIES THAT WOULD RATHER OUTSMART THE COMPETITION THAN OUTSPEND THEM.

"If you're spending money on advertising, you've probably wondered: Is anybody out there listening?" the ad stated. "Instead of trying to outspend the competition, why not try to outthink them? With messages so interesting that even the most indifferent consumer will stop and look. . . . At Fallon McElligott Rice we believe . . . that imagination is one of the last remaining legal means you have to gain an unfair advantage over your competition. . . . If you are beginning to have some questions about whether anybody out there is listening to your advertising, perhaps you should talk to us. Soon. We have a lot of ideas, a lot of energy and a lot to prove." At the bottom of the page was the agency's phone number.

Certainly the ad was provocative. It set a very high standard for the agency in those early days. Fortunately, the four guys in button-down shirts and the woman with the sweet smile and long hair were able to match the bravado of those words with strong ideas for clients—from those as small as the local Episcopal church to those as large as US West. Their ads right away began winning national awards, and within a few years people in New York were talking about Fallon McElligott Rice in Minneapolis, Leo Burnett in Chicago, and Chiat/Day in Los Angeles as the only three non–New York agencies capable of challenging—and occasionally beating—Madison Avenue creativity.

HOW BIG DO WE GET BEFORE WE GET BAD?

Agencies definitely feel a change in wind when they pass the $100 million mark. Besides opening the way to bigger accounts (starting in the $15 to $30 million range), this milestone allows the agency to begin competing for (if it hasn't already) national and some of the smaller global accounts. Suddenly, the agency finds itself coming under pressure to open more offices. Clients want their agencies to be no more than a two- to three-hour plane ride away. They want quick service and ease of contact. If they are in retail, they may also want the agency to have a web of field offices capable of measuring the impact of new campaigns within weeks, if not days or hours, of their launch.

Agencies have to decide whether they're going to succumb to this pressure. Leo Burnett, at least in the United States, reached $3 billion in billings without opening a full-service office outside its Chicago headquarters. Goodby so far has resisted the pressure to open in New York. But the pressure from clients and new business prospects is relentless.

Some agencies have tried to expand and bought only grief. Boston-based Hill, Holliday has maintained an office in New York for 25 years and never seen it grow past the $100 million mark, until in 2002 when it acquired and merged with the New York office of Frank-furt Balkind Partners. Fallon has had a New York shingle since 1995, but the internal debate about whether the office should maintain its own creative department or use the stronger creative resources of its home office in Minneapolis continues to this day. Deutsch opened offices in Los Angeles and Boston—but not long after, had to close its Boston outpost.

The issue facing agency managers is whether they have the time and inclination to be on planes integrating services between offices and ensuring a constancy of quality and culture. In general, branch offices are to be avoided. Today, technology has given agencies options that allow them to avoid this trap. Agnieszka Winkler, founder of the now defunct Winkler Advertising, went so far as to establish a global digital network of freelance account plan-ners. She built proprietary software that allowed her to test ideas in

20 global markets within 48 hours—without opening a single office outside her San Francisco headquarters.

HOW SOON CAN WE PUT UP THE FOR SALE SIGN?

Agencies are started on dreams. Many of those dreams involve fame and fortune. Unfortunately, the gold rush days appear to be over. Though the top five agency holding companies—WPP Group (WPP), Omnicom, Interpublic Group (IPG), Publicis Groupe, and Havas/Euro RSCG—are under constant pressure to grow their revenue base, the multiples they pay for acquisitions and their appetite for buying new companies have diminished. Occasionally, an acquisition will grab the headlines—like IPG's $267 million purchase of Deutsch in 2000. Deutsch, which claimed $1.5 billion in billings at the time of the sale, was reportedly paid an almost unthinkable multiple of 18 times earnings. Most acquisitions, according to advertising lawyer Rick Kurnit, are lucky to realize 5 or 6 times earnings.

What many agency owners don't realize is that the exorbitant sums being offered are easily dissipated—and in most cases, are actually less than what the agency could have generated over the earn-out period had it stayed independent.

At about the same time that Deutsch was being purchased in New York, the partners of a midranked San Francisco shop billing about $300 million, Citron Haligman Bedecarre, decided to cede control of the agency to an investor allied with the global consultancy Accenture. The agency was valued in the $50 to $70 million range. The partners were paid mostly in stock, not cash. In addition, they were committed to invest the cash they did raise toward the purchase of a series of interactive shops, which would make them an international digital marketing communications agency.

Cofounder Kirk Citron says his goal had always been to sell the agency one day. But within two years of the sale, after the agency had been subsumed by one of the interactive agencies it purchased, London-based AKQA, two of the three original partners had left or been forced out, most of the agency's San Francisco staff had been laid off, and the new agency was a shadow of its former self.

CHANGING FROM A THREE-YEAR TO A THREE-MONTH CYCLE

Keith Reinhard, worldwide chief of the DDB network, with offices in 96 countries, says when he looks at a potential acquisition, he doesn't start with the financials. "The first thing we ask is whether we like the people. That's number one. At end of this process, his financial guy and my financial guy are going to hammer out the deal. But first we've got to really like each other and agree where the business is going and what are the best ideas for the future," Reinhard says.

"Once they've passed that test, we want to know what kind of work they are doing and what kind of place they are running. Are their people happy? When I look at their work, do I think, '*Wow*, I'd like to have that on the DDB reel.' Then we get to the practical part. For instance, if 85 percent of his business will be lost if they join us, then maybe we have to find some other way to be friends or affiliates under a different brand."

The profits from such a sale are usually deceptive. (See Rick Kurnit's Seller's Checklist.) Agencies are valued based on a number of factors—profits, growth rate, the longevity of their top clients, the agency's creative reputation, the client experience of the partners, and so on. An agency throwing off, say, $2 million in profit a year for four years may be worth $8 to $10 million—providing the key players agree to stay on for another four years and accept being indentured through an earn-out agreement that pays them the bulk of the purchase price, conditional on the agency maintaining a specified profit level.

Rick Kurnit's Seller's Checklist

✔ Are you ready to take a salary for your day-to-day contribution?

✔ How much control will you have during the earn-out? Must you have the last call over staff, bonuses and compensation, pitch prospects, and so on in order to hit your earn-out targets?

✔ What types of control will you gradually hand over to the buyer? Will you let the new owner change the agency's name? Move back-office functions to another unit to pare costs? Direct your new-business prospecting? Integrate subsidiaries into sibling entities?

✔ Will the buyer give you any new capabilities to boost your new business and client service efforts?

✔ What extra compensation will you receive, if any, if the agency outdistances profit goals during the earn-out?

✔ What compensation do you need for losing any accounts due to conflicts after the deal is consummated?

✔ What is your exit strategy at the end of the earn-out? Are you comfortable with what the buyer proposes in the way of long-term employment guarantees?

The cash in a buyout can be illusory. After all, if any agency is profitable and growing, it might make more on year-on-year earnings than through a sale. Let's say profits are growing at the rate of 20 percent a year. The agency's profit, calculated on a compounded formula over five years, would amount to $10 million—not to mention the extra $1 million it could have earned on its money had it been invested. Meanwhile, profit aside, if billings are growing so well, the agency actually might be worth twice the original offered price, simply because during the growth phase, agency revenues and profits tend to accelerate. Unless someone offered $16 to $20 million, it might be better for the partners to turn down the offer and stay independent.

These are all financial issues, but other factors might motivate agency owners to sell. Most agencies are started by entrepreneurs— and creatively oriented ones at that. They relish their independence and generally hate reporting to bosses and bureaucracies. It's their very independence that probably drew clients to them in the first place. As soon as they sell, they are suddenly confronted by hard-headed CFOs and even less sympathetic stock analysts who care little about the Clios in the lobby trophy case or the special needs of loyal clients. They want to see costs kept to a minimum and quarterly profit goals met. A number of formerly independent agency CEOs can tell you of the cold fury they felt the first time they received a call from a holding company's human resources director telling them not to raise salaries more than 3 percent or give Christmas bonuses.

If money is not a factor, it's hard to find a reason to sell a success-ful small- to medium-sized agency—unless one of your big clients is demanding that you establish offices in distant markets or you need help with below-the-line services and other resources you can't develop on your own.

This is not to say that all such sales immediately degrade the value of the purchased company or that holding companies and acquiring agencies don't try to nurture their acquisitions and maintain their special qualities after a sale. It's a difficult high-wire act for both sides. But in the end, the acquirer has no choice. Without profits and growth in its subsidiaries, its own balance sheet and equilibrium will be destabilized. No publicly held company—let alone a marketing communications company—has a slush fund big enough to under-write the mistakes of an acquisition for very long.

Even if the parent can protect an underperforming business unit for a quarter or two, eventually the pressure of the marketplace is felt. Shareholders and lien holders in privately held companies eventually run out of patience, too, of course, but not as quickly or with such severity.

In trying to maintain a growth path through the earn-out period, both sides need to remind themselves of why the sale was attempted in the first place. Agency owners should have very clear objectives in seeking a sale. If they have to cash out or pay off a departing partner, if they need new capabilities or want cash for expansion and acquisi-tions, then maybe a sale is worth the grief.

If the acquiring agency sees real value in the purchase—if it's a good strategic fit and expands its capabilities in terms of servicing a core client or moving into a new field or geographic area—then the purchase should create long-term value even if it isn't able to realize the hoped-for profit in the early years.

That's what agency mergers are for. The new whole should equal more than the sum of the individual parts. Without some risk, it would just be a matter of flipping a switch and watching the money machine churn out cash.

Conversely, agencies that are in trouble would do better to work through their problems than to turn to buyers for solutions. As fishing writer Tom Henderson has said, seeking shelter in a storm may be a way of keeping dry—but you don't bag trout from under a rain tent.

LEADERSHIP LESSONS FOR DEALING WITH THE SINE WAVE OF AGENCY LIFE

✔ Agencies are just another form of small business. Start with a business plan that charts at least two years of expenses and potential revenue. If your model doesn't turn a profit in a year or two years of growth—don't bother.

✔ Don't think of starting an agency unless you have enough cash to fund six months without any revenue. You don't have to have an account to start an agency—but you have to have enough cash to hold on until you win one.

✔ There is no magic mix for starting an agency, but certainly it takes someone with a flair for creativity paired with someone who has good business sense.

✔ As soon as possible, hire a professional part-time or full-time business manager to keep you on the straight and narrow.

✔ Sooner or later you're going to have to invest in strategic resources. These include account planning and, for some, strategic planning. Don't stint on these critical forms of intellectual capital—but don't feel in the beginning everyone has to be working full-time, either.

✔ A year into the life of a new agency, or about the time it passes the $15 to $25 million mark, the owners should realize it has come of age. Rethink everything at this point to be sure you're on a good path.

✔ Also begin as early as you can making an annual allocation to the rainy day fund. Banks don't like to extend credit to struggling agencies. You may have to bootstrap it. Clients come and go. But you're building a business and a brand that should be able to survive a storm or two.

✔ When you pass the $50 million mark or find that you now have 30 or more employees, do another rethink. You're about to outgrow your local client base and qualify for $10 million national-level accounts. Ask yourself if that's a game you want to play and whether you have the resources to play it successfully.

✔ The next milestone will be $100 million in billings. At that level you can begin to look over the horizon. You are in an elite group. Is your creative product competitive? What makes you distinctive? Is any one account so large that its departure will put you in jeopardy? Do you need more than one office? Do you have too many small (below $2 million) accounts that are overburdening staff and fragmenting your resource base? Which categories are still open and need to be filled?

✔ The final clear milestone will come at around the $300 to $400 million mark. Now you are reaching the top rank of agencies. How are you going to go any higher? What if some of your leading clients want to grow overseas? Are they interested in continuing to buy media through you, or are they ready to graduate to an unbundled model? From here on, it becomes very difficult to fund and manage growth by yourself. This is the time to analyze closely the pluses and minuses of linking up with one of the great global networks.

✔ Every three or four years, go on a retreat with your partners, perhaps even hiring an outside facilitator to conduct it, and reexamine all the premises of your agency. Is it time to reengineer your systems and architecture? Are you organized properly for the future? Is there some function in the agency, like account service or media buying, that could be totally restructured or done away with? Is there some new service (e.g., event marketing, strategic planning, or design) that you want to access but that would be better built on a separate P&L under a separate brand?

✔ Remember, form in agency life does not have to equal substance, but form certainly influences substance. Stay true to your agency's mission and culture, and be brutal about redrawing everything else when necessary.

✔ If you do consider a sale, be prepared to open the agency's books to prospective buyers. Be sure you know the reasons for going after a sale. They have to be compelling—otherwise, you might be better off pocketing the dividends or selling your share to your present partners.

✔ Agency brands should represent enduring values, but they have to be built of sturdy materials. If your line is tired with age or gunky, then it's time to refit your rig.

CHAPTER 8

Smart Ownership Principles

Fish sense, applied in the field, is what the old Zen masters would call enlightenment: simply the ability to see what's right there in front of you without having to sift through a lot of thoughts and theories and yes, expensive fishing tackle.

John Gierach
Trout Bum[1]

The moment of truth for an agency comes when it's time to sell it. At that time the dreams of the founders are put to the test. It's possible for a young, growing agency to attract many suitors. But there are few fixed assets involved. An agency's real value comes from its client relationships, its employees, and the quality of its brand. Clients and employees can't be nailed to the floor. They can walk out as soon as the sale is announced. So the owners have a lot to consider.

It's only good fish sense to compensate your key employees with part of the profits each year as a just reward for their efforts—and then arrange for them to have some participation in the rising equity of an agency as it grows. This becomes especially important when an agency is offered for sale, because a buyer is going to expect most of these employees and the accounts they serve to remain, at least through the three to five years of the standard earn-out. Merely offering top people a salary—when the owners may be anticipating in a huge payoff—is a recipe for disaster.

Experts in brokering agencies say that the time to prepare for the sale is when you start an agency. Rick Kurnit, of New York law firm Frankfurt Kurnit Klein & Selz, who is a fixture on Madison Avenue, believes that how the founders construct basic ownership is perhaps the biggest single factor in determining an agency's later salability.

"The cardinal principal for the owner of the agency is to remember that you can't fire your partners or your lease," Kurnit says. "So who you make a true partner is the most important decision, given the vagaries of the advertising business. You can always ratchet back all the way down to being a consultant or the freelance creative team that you were when you started, but you can't change the ownership of the agency without full agreement of all the principals."

Kurnit recommends that anyone other than the original partners be given *phantom equity* rather than real equity as the agency matures. This has the advantage of reassuring new partners that they will participate in the sale and enjoy a percentage of the equity they are building without the burden of them or the agency having to pay for their shares with after-tax dollars.

Phantom equity involves providing employees with a contract that guarantees them a certain percentage of the sale price—providing they are still with the agency at the time of sale. It can also confer on phantom shareholders a percentage of the annual profits. Ideally, it also defines in a "buy-sell clause" how the phantom shares will be valued should the shareholder decide to leave the agency prior to a sale.

The partnership principle was created to give people a real stake in an agency and to pay them back for all their hard work. Partners and top employees are usually given rich bonuses in good years and asked to forgo such bonuses in lean years. But they often are persuaded to remain at an agency with the understanding that when it's sold the value of their shares will skyrocket.

Successful agencies like Kirshenbaum Bond, Goodby, Silverstein & Partners, and Messner Vetere Berger McNamee Schmetterer were started by the highly motivated partners whose names are on the door, but, over time, the founders came to acknowledge the agency's debt to others who followed later. To reward these latecomers, they made them partners, contractual or otherwise.

These partners were then invited to serve on the board of directors, to have access to the agency's books, and to be given leadership on accounts. In many cases, the new partners were given phantom equity so that the agency did not have to pay for stock bestowed on them with after-tax dollars. (The partners were not considered by the tax law to have received anything tangible at the time of the award.)

Phantom stock is not regarded as income at the time of issuance. The government agrees to wait until the agency is sold, at which time it taxes the difference between book value and market value as ordinary income (not as a capital gain). Likewise, the agency, because it had not given or sold a portion of its value at the time of the phantom award, does not have to buy back its stock with after-tax dollars.

Besides avoiding the 30 percent cut expected by Uncle Sam for any formal transfer of ownership, the seller is able to maintain more control over the company, and the recipient is able to achieve almost all the benefits of real stock ownership.

"Agencies should not simply assume that they are like other companies with hard assets and a minimum value to their equity. In fact, they're just the opposite," says Kurnit. "Everything is ephemeral. And the agency is at risk of being eaten alive, if it has to repeatedly buy back stock of employees with after-tax dollars.

"Is there another way? Absolutely. Phantom equity removes tax accountants and lawyers from all interim transactions while still achieving the key purpose of owning equity—the right to receive a percentage of the sale price when the agency is sold if you are still there. If the principals wish to give the recipient some control over the agency during their tenure or a share of annual profits—the two other attributes of equity—they can do so by the employment agreement that every key employee should sign." (See Kurnit's Incoming Partner Checklist.)

WHAT KIND OF POT OF GOLD ARE WE TALKING ABOUT?

People seeking employment in the top positions of growing and healthy agencies can ask for a lot of concessions short of ownership. By far the biggest lure is equity. That is because agencies with margins above 15 percent are typically valued at multiples of five times profits in the year that they are sold.

Rick Kurnit's Incoming Partner Employment Checklist

✔ Equity

✔ Salary

✔ Signing bonus (to make up for any bonuses, profit sharing, or vesting lost in leaving your prior employment)

✔ Bonus (minimum)

✔ Long-term incentive plan (phantom equity)

✔ Deferred compensation (vesting)

✔ Duration (i.e., minimum period of contract)

✔ Severance
  • Term plus lump sum
  • Lump sum = X months of salary
  • No reduction for other income over X months of salary
  • Mitigated by other income earned
  • Bridging until new employment
  • Notice of termination date

✔ Narrowly define cause so that termination for poor performance still triggers severance

✔ Title, responsibilities, reporting chain—so that a material diminution constitutes constructive termination and triggers right to receive severance

✔ Noncompete/nonsolicitation of clients and employees

✔ Confidentiality of agency and client information

✔ Indemnification against claims by former employer

✔ Benefits
  • Health, execucare, dental
  • Life—extra
  • Disability—extra
  • Car, garage, maintenance
  • Tax counseling
  • Business development budget
  • Clubs
  • First-class travel
  • 401(k)

✔ Attorney's fee

Equity may seem like a magnificent bonus for working in the advertising business, but it, too, can be illusory. Most contracts of sale are qualified by the requirement that the selling agency continue to realize the same margin of profits during the earn-out period. Even though the owners may be given a down payment on the purchase price, the actual price paid by the buyer will depend on profits three to five years after the sale.

Meanwhile, if profits fall during the earn-out period—either because clients decide to cut back on their advertising or because of changes in key personnel or conflicts that cause the selling agency to lose valuable clients—the actual price paid to buy the agency may drop. Also, unless the contract of sale has been written to give the seller protection, the buyer immediately takes title to the new agency and has the right to control hiring and compensation, which may burden the agency with unproductive employees or unprofitable assignments.

"The key thing for the seller is to think about who is controlling the company during the earn-out," says Kurnit. "The contract should be written to ensure that incumbent management manages the earn-out, which means, unless profits fall off completely, the sellers retain control over hiring, firing, staffing, pitching, and pricing.

"Otherwise, the holding company can gut your earn-out. They can stick a bunch of high-priced people on your payroll, make you do work for their clients at their return on investment and make you run around pitching business for the holding company, instead of watching the ball. Any one of these actions could make your earn-out go by the wayside. Control during the earn-out is the big issue, because the buyer has to have a reasonable assurance that you're going to protect what is now its asset. And you want assurance that the buyer will let you manage the earn-out so you realize your full value. Frankly, there's no right formula—and both sides need to negotiate this issue in good faith."

All of these issues should give someone invited into the ownership circle reason to pause. It's possible to write a partnership contract with certain protections for star employees—but shareholders have to share in the upsides and downsides. Still, there is tremendous value assigned to equity. The reason is simple. Consider the following typical agency valuation on sale.

Agency A (15% Margin and Stagnant)

Billings: $200 million

Gross revenue: $30 million

Income: $4.5 million

Valuation 4 × earnings: $18 million

However, if an agency is able to achieve margins of much more than 15 percent, it may be valued at five, six, or seven times earnings.

Agency B (20% Margins and Growing)

Billings: $200 million

Gross revenue: $30 million

Income: $6 million:

Valuation 6 × earnings: $36 million

A partner with a 10 percent share who is taking home a salary of $200,000 a year and a bonus in good years of another $200,000, may expect, in the case of Agency A, to receive $1.8 million and, in the case of Agency B, $3.6 million—merely because the second agency is better managed. But that payoff assumes that in the five years of the earn-out the agency will continue to produce the 15 or 20 percent margins declared at the time of the sale. However, if the agency craters, the payoff could be much smaller—perhaps $340,000 in the first year and $100,000 or so in following years.

WHAT OTHER CHOICES DO OWNERS HAVE FOR ARRANGING AN ELEGANT EXIT?

All the experts warn against selling without a very good reason.

"You need to understand that the only time it makes sense to sell is when you hit a wall," says Kurnit. "When you no longer can grow without a major infusion of cash or a major addition of capabilities, because what you get for your asset is going to be a function of your profits, which are in turn a function of your margins and your size. So you have to ask yourself if you won't make more just taking home your profits each year in the form of bonuses."

Of course, there comes a time when even old goats have to retire and hand off control to a new generation. At that point they have to arrange to sell their shares to the second tier. This group, unless they have access to other capital, must generally make payments for the agency out of future profits. Again, the old owners are facing an earn-out, but instead of being paid by a publicly owned holding company with deep pockets, they are being paid by their former employees. This again depends on the vagaries of the market but it still might be a better choice than selling to a company that is going to change the soul of your business and regard it merely as an office of a national or international network.

John Anderson's Checklist for Prospective Buyers[2]

✔ Is the agency known for its strong creative services or some other element that differentiates it from the competition and ensures it some chance of success?

✔ Does the agency have a written business plan that shows its owners have planned their growth—and are they keeping to it?

✔ Is the agency a real business? Has it been making its margins of 15 percent or more for several years? Are the principals being guided by a financial director or outside accountant who successfully keeps expenses from outdistancing revenues.

✔ Are the owners of the agency covered by a sensible shareholder agreement that makes it possible for them to sell the agency without too much rancor from minority shareholders?

✔ Has the agency been successful in helping current clients grow their business—and, as a result, clients are increasing ad budgets year by year?

✔ When it goes after new business, is it successful, and do the new clients bond? Looking at the last five clients to leave the agency—were they seeking better service, or was separation caused by more benign factors?

✔ What kinds of conflicts will the acquisition create? Is there enough value after certain clients leave the agency to make the acquisition still worthwhile?

✔ Will the owners agree to stay on during the earn-out? When they do peel off, is there a good second layer of management ready to take their place?

✔ Culture: Does the acquired agency embrace the same values as the buyer? Will they one day be able to merge their businesses without too much dissidence?

✔ Value: Have the owners of the business taken a reasonable stance toward valuing their agency?

Meanwhile, agencies continue to be sold, because the publicly owned massive holding companies need to increase revenues to maintain their stock price, and buying revenue is usually easier than growing it through the growth of current assets.

Of course, selling is not inevitable. It's just that 90 percent of the great agencies reach a point where that seems a smart next step. It's for that reason that even agencies determined to remain independent should be built on a flexible foundation that expands rather than contracts options.

LEADERSHIP LESSONS FOR PROSPECTIVE AGENCY OWNERS

✔ Create a basic partnership agreement that includes sensible ways for the partnership to dissolve if friction occurs or if the agenda of one of the partner's changes.

✔ Try to avoid diluting control as the agency grows. Later partners should be allowed to achieve their goals through phantom equity rather than real equity.

✔ Create a one-, two-, and/or three-year business plan that all the partners embrace. Revise it every one or two years to keep it timely.

✔ If you decide to distribute equity to employees, make it clear whether they are getting a share in the capitalization of the agency (i.e., profits on sale), a share in the profits year by year, or actual control over the agency's management and access to its books.

✔ Create an executive bonus pool separate from your equity pool that allows you to offer bonuses to top performers regardless of their ownership.

✔ Try to avoid selling the agency unless it's clear that you have reached a barrier in growth; that you need capabilities a buyer might offer; and/or that you need to cash out one or all of the partners who want to retire or leave the agency.

✔ Be sure in an earn-out that you are given sufficient control over the agency to give you a reasonable chance of meeting your profit goals.

✔ Ensure that the agency's name is protected as ownership changes over time.

✔ Determine how partners who leave early can sell back their stock to the agency. Will it be valued at book or market value?

✔ If agency profits should crater during the earn-out, specify how the agency might buy itself back from the new owner.

CHAPTER 9

Integrating and Refocusing the Agency Network

To paraphrase Heraclitus, you can never fish in the same river twice. Conditions are always different, minute by minute, cast by cast, and the ability to adjust to changing conditions—to instruct yourself quickly—is a good measure of an angler's success.

Verlyn Kinkenborg

Sports Afield, August 1996[1]

For many in the advertising world, 1986 will always be remembered as the year of the Big Bang. I recall it well because at the time I was editor of the Southeastern edition of *Adweek* and was summoned to a trade association meeting to serve on a panel evaluating this milestone. We weren't exactly sure what it meant, but we knew that the tectonic plates of the ad world had shifted.

The Big Bang referred to the decision of the owners of BBDO, DDB, and Needham Harper Steers to merge their stock into a single holding company, Omnicom, and essentially become one giant global advertising company. They were not the first. The Interpublic Companies (IPG) had been formed by Marion Harper in 1960, taking with it McCann-Erickson, still the largest agency in the United States. Later it purchased Lintas, the giant agency built to manage Unilever's many brands, and Frank Lowe's The Lowe Group.

The Big Bang was a big deal because it signaled the beginning of the final consolidation of the global advertising business. The motivation was service: Agencies were striving to be better at serving global clients, which themselves were rapidly consolidating into two or three companies at the top of each category. However, it was perceived as a money play. Clients were already wary of the profits that agencies were making on their business, especially after the sale by Bob Jacoby of Bates to the Saatchi brothers for the unheard of price of just over $450 million.

The Bates sale and the Big Bang pushed many clients over the edge. Instead of paying 15 percent commissions on the media placed by their agencies and not being sure how that financed the work of agencies, they were determined to switch to a fee basis whereby agency work could be more precisely measured. In the beginning, the fees were comparable to 14 or 15 percent commissions. Over time, fees were cut back until today many of the larger companies are paying in the neighborhood of 8 to 10 percent.

Meanwhile, agency consolidation has continued apace. Omnicom has since bought TBWA and Chiat/Day and merged the two. True North was formed out of the carcasses of Foote, Cone & Belding and Bozell—and then sold to Interpublic.

Martin Sorrell, formerly chief financial officer of the Saatchis' amazing empire, set out to create his own holding company, WPP Group. His first purchase was J. Walter Thompson, followed by Ogilvy & Mather, then more recently by Young & Rubicam.

French-based Havas purchased Messner Vetere Berger McNamee Schmetterer in New York, Dahlin Smith White in Salt Lake, and Tatham Laird in Chicago to form another network, under a company created by a merger of two largely French agency networks, Euro and RSCG.

Then, a few years ago, Bcom3 was formed by forging Leo Burnett, D'Arcy Masius Benton & Bowles, and an investment from Japanese giant Dentsu. Paris-based Publicis Groupe, led by Maurice Levy, who already owned Hal Riney, Fallon, and Saatchi, formed the world's fourth biggest holding company in 2002 by buying Bcom3.

U.S.-based brands like Fallon; Goodby, Silverstein & Partners; Hill, Holliday, Connors, Cosmopulos; Mullen; The Martin Agency; Martin/Williams; Bozell; Campbell-Ewald; Carmichael Lynch; Deutsch; Arnold; Ayer; and GSD&M were all swept into the major holding companies. Today the only global agencies operating independently are Grey, Bates, Dentsu, Leagas Delaney, and Wieden + Kennedy. Though there is some curiosity about what plays are left for these five top global independents, the great consolidation of the 1980s and 1990s can be said to be now largely complete.

If you are a global client like Ford, whose brands—including Jaguar, Land Rover, and Volvo—are almost all at WPP agencies,[2] you have very few choices left. William Ford Jr. can move his car accounts from one WPP agency to another, but if he goes outside the WPP family of agencies he will bump into competitors like General Motors, whose brands are almost all at Interpublic,[3] or DaimlerChrysler, whose brands are all at Omnicom.

Agencies are trapped, too. If Ford wishes to reduce its fees to J. Walter Thompson, WPP's Martin Sorrell would have a hard time explaining to shareholders why he fired the client—because other of his agencies depend on Ford for their major car accounts. It's kind of like a Monopoly game where all the prime properties are taken. Now it's just a matter of piling on houses and hotels to decide who is going to be the big winner.

WHAT DO CLIENTS WANT?

With all the pieces in play, now the real game begins. It's not so much a matter of winning new accounts but of ramping up the total revenues from each client. Holding companies are concentrating now on trying to get more of a client's business (i.e., the relatively smaller fees their global clients are paying for below-the-line services). WPP would seem to have top-of-the-hill honors in the field of public relations, by owning both Burson Marstellar and Hill & Knowlton, two of the world's largest PR agencies. Interpublic has the lead in promotions by owning Momentum. The direct-marketing category is led by Wunderman, another WPP brand, but the global purse on direct marketing has been fragmented by customer relationship management (CRM) monies being reallocated to the Internet, where no holding company holds sway.

Media is turning out to be its own separate battleground, as more and more clients unbundle media buying—that is, take it from their creative agency and reassign it to a global media buying company owned by one of the five great holding companies. The leaders are Starcom MediaVest (Publicis), Initiative (Interpublic), Optimum (Omnicom), and Optimedia (WPP). Zenith, another big media company, is currently jointly owned by Publicis and Cordiant, parent to Bates, but it is assumed Publicis will soon buy the remaining half from

Cordiant. The only global company without a media company of such global size is Euro RSCG, which is planning acquisitions to cure that problem.

But the holding companies still have one more card to play. Some feel the growth in fees in the future will come from strategic planning. It's an open question now whether those fees will go to one of the great agencies, to small strategic marketing companies formed or purchased by the holding companies, or to one of the well-established independents, companies like Accenture, Booz Allen, Boston Consulting, and McKinsey, which are increasingly focusing on marketing assignments and are rushing to build their own resource base in this area.

There are also questions regarding who will integrate (or, in the argot of the day, *orchestrate*) the growing array of marketing services. Agencies believe that because they own the various pieces of the marketing mix—advertising, PR, interactive, promotions, media, direct marketing—they will be asked to integrate services for their clients. However, many advertisers, who think agencies are tasked just getting all their offices in sync, are either taking responsibility for the integration function or parceling it out to third-party providers.

THE GLOBAL CULTURE MYTH

Agency leaders will tell you their networks are connected by a global culture. At every Leo Burnett office you will find a bowl of apples in the reception area. In Ogilvy offices, 20 years ago, men wore red suspenders. In fact, agency chiefs have enough trouble putting out an occasional newsletter, let alone defining the network's culture. The question of how to describe DDB's worldwide culture seems to catch chairman Keith Reinhard by surprise. "At DDB we believe creativity is the most powerful force in business. An idea well conceived and implemented can transform the world," he says. "Out of that point of view comes our promise: Anywhere you go in the DDB world, you will get better ideas that will produce better results."

By now the words have descended into hyperbole. But in a later discussion, Reinhard concedes that forging a common culture, between the offices of Needham and DDB, was hard enough. Trying to spin it out through a global network is incredibly difficult. "Our basic tenet," he says "is that the stronger the culture, the less need for structure. And in order to attract highly creative entrepreneurs to our network we need the absence of rigid, centralized structures. So we developed a 'no rules' philosophy.

"We ask that all 12,000 people in the DDB network embrace the creative philosophy of Bill Bernbach, our founder, and we charge our managers with applying that philosophy in whatever ways are appropriate to their local market and national culture. To emphasize that point, we say that, 'rules are for people who don't know what to do.' The heads of our offices around the world are leaders who know what to do."

Shared values and common goals are disseminated in various ways. Reinhard writes a newsletter, *Any Wednesday*. In addition, he and his designated successor and current president, Ken Kaess, conduct a "Ken and Keith" session with young executives from DDB offices four times a year. "We're trying to say what you do in Estonia matters as much as what your colleagues in Paris or New York are doing," says Reinhard.

Reinhard has built his network by attracting strong entrepreneurs whose agencies lead in their local markets, people such as Nizan Guanes, of DM9 DDB in Brazil; Frank Palmer, of Palmer Jarvis DDB in Canada; and Pietro Tramontin, of Results DDB in Holland. Such advertising leaders don't take kindly to too much direction from New York. So Reinhard's no-rules philosophy relies on each office in the network knowing what's best for a brand in that country.

"*Management* is probably the wrong word for our culture," says Reinhard. "The root word for *manage* has to do with getting horses to obey commands. We depend on smart, talented people who don't need to be managed so much as guided, inspired, and rewarded."

In such a no-rules environment, one should expect brilliant if sometimes uneven executions—making it more difficult at times for a global client to enforce a global message. Some clients, of course, see a benefit in this loose approach. It gives more power to their own local marketing directors to adapt their global positioning to the local culture. But others chafe at this somewhat chaotic approach.

A RULES-DRIVEN CULTURE

TBWA under Jean-Marie Dru, on other hand, is fairly fanatical about culture. Dru first published his book *Disruption* in 1996 before he took over as president of TBWA.[4] In the intervening years, it has become the mantra of every TBWA office. With the sequel, *Beyond Disruption*, whose chapters detail actual case histories by various office managers, the theory has become so ingrained in the network's work that it is even starting to find its way, literally, into its advertising—as with the new Nissan "shift" campaign.[5]

"The reason I wanted Jean-Marie Dru to be my partner when we were deciding who's on top of this new merged entity is that he's a very passionate guy," says Lee Clow, who serves as chairman and worldwide creative director of the network. "Disruption is an edgy, passionate way to think about what we do as opposed to a safe-and-sane, everything-in-moderation, kind of strategy. We keep trying to attract the best people that we can. And we tell them our goal is still to change the rules, do something different. Do something brave, change the world."

Clow had to pay special attention to issues of culture during the merger, because Chiat/Day at the time was perceived as an embattled entity that had been losing key clients and people under the stress of the early-1990s recession and some of Jay Chiat's poor business decisions.

"There's been some very ugly ones," says Clow of the big mergers. He cites the demise of Ammirati Puris, which lost its spirit and eventually many of its clients when it was merged with Lintas—even though Martin Puris was given control of the new brand, Ammirati Puris Lintas. Doyle Dane and Needham was a very rocky merger for many years—especially for the shell of Doyle Dane in New York. The bitterness of the partisans for Compton and Dancer Fitzgerald Sample, when those two agencies were merged into what became Saatchi

& Saatchi in the United States, is another example of a difficult combination.

"I thought it was a very, very right thing to do for the company," says Clow of the merger of TBWA and Chiat/Day. "Jay wasn't quite so on board. But his anxiety had more to do with some financial pressures that weren't allowing us to reward some people and things like that. I felt we had to do this but we had to try to do it right, and do it on our terms, and not lose our soul and not lose our vision."

Oddly enough, this one merger of two very strong, different cultures seems to have worked to the benefit of both agencies, with a minimum of bloodletting. TBWA in the United States wasn't known as a very interesting creative agency—with the exception of its brilliant print campaign for Absolut. Chiat/Day had struggled to establish a presence in New York and was on the rocks financially. Today the two parts see themselves as one agency, though there remains some residual tension between TBWA New York and Chiat/Day's Los Angeles office.

"Interestingly," says Clow, "I happened to be talking to [then Omnicom chairman] Bruce Crawford about my optimism about the thing—and he said something cryptic to me like, 'Well, that's nice, but every merger has winners and losers.'

"Of course, TBWA was already an Omnicom company and Chiat/Day was being acquired. But I think we stayed true to ourselves. After all, we kept the Chiat/Day brand [in the name of the Los Angeles office]. And we kind of negotiated how we put it all together, just like Hunt Lascaris [in South Africa] and some of the other TBWA companies remained as distinct subbrands. We just went about our work, looking for some kind of proof that we weren't going to become subsumed or consumed by this merger and evaporate. And we ended up being the emotional lead of the new merged company."

Meanwhile, TBWA became known again in Europe and other parts of the world as a rising creative star. "I think we both ended up achieving what we wanted," says Clow. "Chiat/Day is recognized as something that gave this newly merged company style and attitude, and at the same time, TBWA delivered us a network and the wisdom to not try to suppress the spirit of Chiat/Day."

Most mergers create a network in name only—trying to fuse

cultures, balance sheets, and egos that don't really have much in common with one another. I learned firsthand of the lack of fraternal love in such networks when I was hired recently as a consultant on an agency search for a Fortune 500 company. The U.S.-based client was being served by a European office of one of the top 10 networks. It decided to fire the European agency and wanted the network's New York office to pitch the account. The European agency sent over a senior officer, who at first warned the client against even considering its New York sibling and threatened to refuse to share its knowledge with New York. Later, it backed down from that position, but it was clear that global culture in this network was little more than window dressing.

CAN WE LEARN ANYTHING FROM THE PENTAGON?

In the end, global management of an account is essentially a command-and-control problem, as they say in the military. First the network leader must try to see that every office in the network shares a certain minimum competence. Then it needs to centralize control over the account in a single individual and give that individual say in how the resources of each office are allocated to servicing that account.

This last element is perhaps the most difficult to achieve, because in the end, an office's profit and loss (P&L) is the responsibility of the local CEO. Let's say that JWT's worldwide manager of the Ford business wants to introduce a new campaign for brand Ford to replace "No Boundaries." First the account manager wants to be sure he or she has the right creative and that the client is ready to roll out the campaign idea worldwide. There may be delays while the client's own bureaucracy vets the new line—meanwhile, it has to be tested by account planners in each country where it is to run to be sure there are no hidden negatives (like the time Chevrolet had a problem calling its low-priced offering a Nova, because in Spanish countries *No va* means "can't go").

Then the account manager wants to activate marketing plans by both agency and client in every country to support the rollout. For this, the manager will need the help of a range of services—including planning for local launch parties, TV commercials, outdoor ads, local promotions, direct mail, changes in the local content area of the brand's global Web site, and so on. But in several offices, say, in Kuala Lumpur, Malaysia, and Santiago, Chile, the local account manager on the Ford business may have been reassigned to a new business effort or may be working on something more profitable to the local office, and temporarily at least, the Ford brand team may be without a leader.

Suddenly, the account manager is on the telephone or, more likely in today's world, the Internet, asking for a new team leader. The head of the local office may e-mail back: "Listen, pal, we care about Ford. We know how important it is to the network and WPP. But I have other priorities here. So, no, I'm not going to find you someone else to run the Ford business. Just be patient and we'll work things out."

In this case, of course, the worldwide account manager can then appeal to the head of J. Walter Thompson, Peter A. Schweitzer, or if that doesn't solve the problem he can go to the head of the parent, Martin Sorrell himself. Or, if he is of a mischievous bent, he can slyly tell the client that he isn't sure that the new campaign is going to be rolled out in Malaysia or wherever—and let the client call Schweitzer or Sorrell for satisfaction. Either way, the electricity would move up and down the command channels of both agency and client until the matter was resolved.

But this is an old model not well suited to today's rapidly changing environment. Ideas need to move both into the center and out from the center all the time. Brand team leaders at agencies need to learn how to utilize all their resources—and not seek to control the process as much as orchestrate it. The more you centralize power, the less invested people in local offices are in the process. Quality and creativity will certainly suffer.

Meanwhile, agency CEOs have enough problems coordinating with the holding companies to which they report—let alone managing acquisitions, holding the hands of major clients, worrying about new business, and talking to other important constituencies like the press, agency analysts, consultants, and shareholders. To be spending time on control issues makes little sense.

In a perfect world, Reinhard's decentralized, no-rules philosophy would seem to be the best approach. This way, if you have strong, competent leaders managing each office, they can use their own judgment on what tack to take locally. But this often does not sit well with the client—whose desire for economies of scale and global control was why these global networks were established in the first place. Not all ideas are equal in strength. Someone in the end has to determine the balance between global brand positioning and local content. The referee should come from within the system and ideally be more attuned to the creative side of the process than the business side. Simply empowering account managers to run the process doesn't solve the problem. In fact, because of the traditional account executive's training and background, it probably works to kill the creative process rather than to enhance it.

THE DIGITAL SIDE OF THE PROBLEM

The Internet and the dramatic advances of technology offer some new operational, if not human, forms of control and communication to ensure a more rapid response. Now agencies have the ability to establish intranets to house all of their instructions, text, data, graphics, and whatever for managing the creative side of the account. The sophistication of these programs differs greatly from network to network. At the very minimum, they should provide a single digital file where everyone in the network and even the client can go to view every communication and creative application. This, then, becomes an archive of intellectual property and a way of ensuring that the core equities of a client's brand (the design and color of its logo, the product claims made on its behalf, etc.) are never violated.

Of more importance, these files then can become the *intellectual capital* of an agency—giving it the chance to archive its insights for one client and use them later for others. Case histories, briefs, and tactical defenses against countermeasures of competing brands need to be archived and made available to the rest of the network all the time. By the same token, as this file cabinet of knowledge and insights becomes larger, a Chinese fire wall needs to be erected to ensure that proprietary information is never shared with a competitor—especially in networks where clients tolerate conflicts in different countries.

In BBDO, for instance, the network represents DaimlerChrysler in key markets like the United States. But in Brazil, Almap BBDO does award-winning advertising for Volkswagen. BBDO must manage its digital archive so as to give the new business executives throughout BBDO access to information about how the agency in the United States was able to maximize promotional opportunities for Chrysler without violating the privacy demands of Chrysler by sharing such information with anyone connected with Volkswagen.

WHERE'S THE BIG IDEA?

The challenge for these great networks, though, is not so much control as the development and sharing of good ideas. Global account managers for a brand in these networks may be too focused on issues of security and control. Some are more interested in demonstrating that they can distribute ideas developed in the home office around the world than they are in coming up with new messages that help the client generate sales and keep its brands fresh and appealing.

Clients such as Procter & Gamble have become so gun-shy about a system built to satisfy their own concerns about discipline that they have developed an independent, parallel network for learning about breakthrough communications from distant points. In one case, a Latin agency trying to meet the budget constraints of a local client who wanted a punchy new TV spot for a cleanser came up with the idea of using a handheld camera and an announcer to interview housewives in what appeared to be spontaneous encounters. The rough video quality of the commercial and the offbeat impromptu humor of the announcer, who was actually a professional comedian, gave the spot a quirky freshness that caught people's attention. And the housewives' testimonials seemed real enough to be believed. In the end, P&G instructed its agencies to employ the same approach for advertising the brand around the world.

Meanwhile, the name of the game should be the quality of the idea developed by the network, regardless of origin. What is needed is either a new kind of chief idea officer (CIO) to oversee the development and dissemination of ideas throughout the network or a new kind of global account manager, trained in basic ideation skills and knowledgeable enough to apply these skills to a digital framework. It's one thing to encourage freewheeling ideation in a room with a whiteboard; it's another thing to work with people through a digital network where there is no face-to-face contact and no two offices are necessarily connected at the same time. For many networks, this doesn't require establishing a new position—they can merely repurpose their often underused worldwide creative director to the task.

Account managers have their feet held to the fire so many times over so many details that they quite naturally become control freaks. They need to be weaned of this inclination. Someone needs to act as a referee. To operate properly, the system needs a client schooled in new methods of open communication and willing to agree on a results-based compensation model that rewards breakthrough ideas. Few agencies have taken the time to design better ways to open their networks to ideas. They've upgraded their digital nervous systems, but most of these systems still lack the sophistication of parallel systems on the client side.

THE SEARCH FOR RESTRAINT AT THE TOP

The hardest person to restrain is the most powerful, and that is the chief executive of the holding company. People like Martin Sorrell of WPP, John Wren of Omnicom, and David Bell of Interpublic have to decide whether they are going to force their networks to share new methods of archiving and sharing information or to stand by and watch each network develop its own.

Sorrell is probably the most digitally oriented of the leaders of the five great holding companies. He's constantly studying new approaches developed at leading business schools, and he has added Esther Dyson, the Internet guru and current head of ICANN, the global Internet agency, to his board to spur WPP's digital leadership. Sorrell himself remains connected to the Internet virtually every waking hour, and stories about the speed with which he answers e-mails—even on weekends and in the evening—are amazing.

If Ogilvy develops its own proprietary idea-sharing software, however, Sorrell might do well to hesitate before ordering it to be shared with his other operating units, because many clients are still counting on the networks to operate autonomously to allow for conflicts within the WPP family. The most that a holding company's chief executive should do in this instance is to celebrate advances by his operating units, while at the same time pressing all of the units to gradually make the transition from an ad focus to an idea focus.

Communication ideas are the most fragile of beasts. They are too easily destroyed by committees and bureaucracies. Agencies need to develop ways to champion ideas so they are guaranteed a fair hearing at the center. It is up to each network to develop systems that overcome all the barriers of distance, culture and time to ensure that good ideas are nurtured and transferred quickly up the chain of command. The other thing these new digital systems should deliver is speed. More and more clients are trying to narrow the time it takes to bring a new product to market. "[Time compression] is simply a condition of doing business in the 21st Century," writes San Francisco technology marketer Agnieszka Winkler, "and there is no option to adjust. Something less than nine months from product concept (not advertising concept) to launch is not unusual."[6]

Agencies now need to learn how to develop campaigns even before a product is fully developed. It takes time to embed a brand name in the public consciousness, but some clients need sales as soon as they come to market. Thus, when Hal Riney was given the assignment to launch Saturn, the agency had to develop a TV campaign without a product shot. It was from this need to get a jump on the competition that led Hal Riney to come up with the line, "A Different Kind of Car. A Different Kind of Company."

The first Saturn ads showed bucolic scenes of Tennessee horse country. The campaign heralded a company that was going to embrace hassle-free sales and Japanese levels of quality, which excited car buyers with the sense that finally a General Motors division was setting new standards for itself. The campaign, devilishly effective with car buyers, managed to enrage the rest of the GM bureaucracy, which later took its vengeance on Saturn by delaying funds for new models for over a decade.

HOW WILL THE NEW COMMITMENT TO IDEAS BE COMMUNICATED?

Any global network agreeing to take on this challenge will initially encounter resistance and confusion. Leaders will probably have to seek help in developing manuals and distributing them. When Jean-Marie Dru wrote his landmark book, *Disruption*, in 1996, he was chairman of the BDDP Group. Soon after the book was published, BDDP was sold to British-owned GGT, but that network struggled and eventually was sold to Omnicom, where it became part of TBWA. In 2001 Dru was named president/CEO and made *Disruption* the idea-generating theory for the whole network. But though the company began developing Disruption workshops for some of its employees as early as 1998 in its Paris and Johannesburg offices, it was not until 2001 that a formal employee manual made it part of the DNA of the network.

Not only must global agencies attack the issue of creating and distributing better ideas for their clients, they must devise new forms of compensation. Time-based fees are a very crude way to reward creativity, but few agencies have been successful in developing alternates.

"As an industry, we haven't made all that much progress in changing the basic approach to compensation," admits Reinhard, who 10 years ago announced a concept, called Guaranteed Results, in which his agency offered to take responsibility for the effectiveness of its work in exchange for a chance to earn a bonus when the work achieved or surpassed objectives.

Reinhard notes that DDB has 30 different kinds of results-based compensation contracts in place, but that, by and large, clients still see advertising as a commodity for which they set the price. "If I had it to do over again, I probably wouldn't have called the idea Guaranteed Results. The word *guarantee* somehow made it sound like a stunt. And we were serious. We were trying to say we'll bet on our creativity to produce real results in the market, and when it does, we want to share in the financial rewards. Even though clients didn't line up at our door at the time, I like to think that our initiative has influenced some degree of compensation reform."

Reinhard hopes that agencies can assume more and more responsibility for defining and building brands and integrating the brand message across all platforms. "Every client will tell you they want a marketing partner. No two of them can agree on what that means," he says. "So we have to understand what they want and customize our service to meet their needs. If all they want is advertising, that's what we'll give them. And we may have to wait awhile before migrating into a consulting relationship with them. But sooner or later, we need to go to a client and say, 'You need a brand analysis to determine where your brand stands relative to your competitors. You need to find out how many friends your brand has and how many lovers. We know how to do that and how to win more lovers for your brand. We know the steps that must be taken to make your brand stronger.' "

Convincing clients to pay for such strategic thinking may be difficult given present agency structures and industry practice. Says Reinhard, "For a period of time we may have to use separately branded units headed by professionals with new skills and new titles. But eventually, once people get used to paying for ideas and consulting, we should be able to put it all back together as one DDB. By 2025, DDB won't stand for just ads. It will stand for all aspects of brand building. But to get from here to there, we'll have to get more creative with nomenclature and subbranding, and we'll have to attract new and different kinds of talents to the company."

LEADERSHIP LESSONS FOR REFOCUSING THE AGENCY NETWORK

✔ Network chiefs have to revisit the issue of culture to ensure a strong creative focus.

✔ Once the mission and approach of the agency have been redefined, networks need internal tools for spreading ideas throughout the network.

✔ Besides workshops and manuals, the Internet is an invaluable tool—not only for setting the tone and goals of agencies within the network but for directing the way a network develops and applies new ideas for its clients

✔ Agency networks have been developed mostly to provide global account managers with control over how creative ideas are distributed and applied. Using such networks for ideation requires new skills, and account managers have to be reschooled in these techniques.

✔ Networks may need to recruit and train a new kind of person—a chief idea officer (CIO)—whose function is parallel to but not quite the same as the knowledge management officer, traditionally charged with the archiving and sharing of information. The function of this chief idea officer bears no relation to that of the chief information officer (CIO), who is basically a technology chief.

✔ Chief idea officers are coaches. Their function amplifies the space currently occupied by the worldwide creative director. Such global creative chiefs originally were charged with helping units within a network come up with better solutions for their clients. In most cases, their role has been limited and marginalized to convening internal creative summit meetings and occasionally replacing local creative directors whose work has been found wanting. In the new era, however, these CIOs will be charged with helping a global account manager develop robust brand solutions and orchestrating the ideation process throughout the network.

✔ Besides refocusing the network on ideas and creating new strategic marketing and strategic planning units, network chiefs will have to evolve new business models. The same barriers to ideation at the agency level are magnified at the network level. If agencies can't charge a premium for their best ideas, then it's unlikely they will be asked to do more than distribute someone else's ideas.

CHAPTER 10

The Future

Opening day of the trout season is the rebirth of an angler's soul.
Roger Menard
My Side of the River[1]

What if the agency of the future is . . . not an ad agency? This is likely to be the case if agencies can't change their spots. The last popular choice for "agency of the future" was Chiat/Day in the early 1990s. Jay Chiat moved its headquarters to a new building designed by Frank Gehry. Instead of everyone having a desk, they had a laptop, a small wall locker, and a phone card. They reported to the concierge who assigned them an area with a phone jack and a power plug. You plugged in your laptop and your phone and away you went. Everything was loaded on servers. Everyone was mobile. And the work—well, the work remained about the same.

Before long the agency ran out of resources and steam and the decision was made to sell the agency to a multinational. After Jay Chiat retired, and the new management arranged for the agency to back out of the lease on the Frank Gehry building and move into more traditional space—where people were again given desks, desktop computers, and desktop telephones.

Today, 10 years later, the Playa del Rey, California, office of Chiat/Day is the creative center of its new owner, TBWA. The work is better. People are happier. But the office is still an ad agency.

We have to look at other kinds of companies—companies currently regarded as outside advertising or seemingly not big enough to threaten the status quo—to see where the business may be heading.

WHAT IF AGENCIES HAD RIGHTS TO THE IDEAS THEY CREATED?

To look for change, start at the edges, in California, where many of the world's trends originate. Here, several small and large agencies bear watching. One is Siltanen/Keehn, located in an airy space in El Segundo. The first thing that strikes you when you walk in the door is the sense of play. Except for some ads on the wall, you could be in the playroom of a rehab center. Off to one side is a small basketball court. Further to the left is a pool table. And everywhere there are toy cars. The cars are reminiscent of the days when the two principals, Rob Siltanen and Pam Keehn, worked on the Nissan account for Chiat/Day.

Siltanen and Keehn believe they are founding a new movement, which they call "advertainment," where ideas are introduced in ads for a brand and then take on a life of their own throughout the culture.

"I guess you could say it all started when we did the 'Toys' campaign for Nissan," explains Siltanen, 39, seated in the room where his wooden conference table is festooned with toy sports cars. "We were approached by Tri-Star about turning the characters from the spot into an animated television series. When I created the spot, I never thought of the characters existing beyond the world of advertising. I was just trying to do the most provocative commercial I could do.

"Then, as the commercial began getting some buzz, I said to myself, 'Wow this is really something.' I realized there was this huge potential coming out of one commercial. *Rolling Stone* magazine has never had a commercial of the year award—ever. Same thing with *Time* magazine. But that year they both made 'Toys' their commercial of the year. I went on *Oprah* to talk about this spot. Jerry Seinfeld was quoted in *Newsweek* saying he was going to give up his show to start an ad agency. Why? Because that Nissan commercial was more talked about than any movie made that year.

"And I thought to myself, 'Whoa! Here's a way to get free PR and provide new revenue streams for clients.' It's about making commercials in a new way to be sure that the idea is fully leveraged through the creative process."

Siltanen began walking the halls of Chiat/Day's very trendy Playa del Rey agency, trying to drum up enthusiasm for investing more time into extending brands through licensed characters.

"We started looking at 'Toys' and asking things like, What if we made remote control cars? And what if we also sold those in the dealerships and through FAO Schwartz and Toys "R" Us? What does that mean as a child growing up and having these really cool cars from Nissan? Doesn't that have some effect on you as you grow up and mature with a brand? And I decided what I was talking about was doing advertising in a form that's better than it's ever been.

"Pam was the account person on the Taco Bell business. The creative team had come up with the commercial with the Chihuahua. Somebody at Taco Bell said 'We're always making toys—why not make the Chihuahua?' In the end, Taco Bell made millions of dollars from the talking Chihuahua toy. Do you know how many tacos you have to sell to make a million bucks?"

Siltanen warms to his argument. "So I started thinking, the model has to change. It's crazy for one agency to be paid like every other agency when that agency might be doing much better work and generating these kind of ideas for the client."

Siltanen had been designated as Lee Clow's successor to be executive creative director of the agency. But as he began to think about what licensing, merchandising, and entertainment spin-offs could do for a brand and what kind of revenue these spin-offs could generate, he became so excited that he and Keehn decided to start their own agency.

From the beginning, they put an emphasis on driving brands with icons and characters that express the personality of a brand and that have the potential for being entertaining in their own right. He believes agencies have a unique ability to use their creativity in this manner because they live in a world that has had to tap into emotions in order to create a bond with the brand.

"We're closer to the consumer, so we understand what makes them laugh or cry," he says. "I already have an understanding, just like any marketing person, of how business works, how a product is supposed to work, and how products fit into a consumer's life. What makes me different is that I'm able to bring those elements closer together than anybody's ever done before and give a client an advantage it never had before. This is what made Jay Chiat the genius that he was. He turned a building into an art form [during the 1984 Los Angeles Olympics] with a Nike athlete on it and having nothing but the swoosh. That was revolutionary. That building became more beautiful with that ad than it ever was without the ad. Yet [the ad] still sold product and spoke to runners everywhere."

Siltanen/Keehn infuses all of its advertising with a special, unique tone of voice and emotion. Oftentimes their campaigns involve characters. For instance, for Round Table pizza, America's fourth-largest pizza chain, Siltanen and Keehn created their own "pizza expert," an easygoing 30-year-old named Billy Sardell who relished the job of tasting pizzas. For Gateway computers, they had founder Ted Waitt conversing with a talking cow, which became an icon in its own right. In some cases, the agency comes up with its own characters and proposes that clients license them. In other cases, it has developed characters for a client's brand and tried to negotiate contract language that would allow it to participate in any income the characters generate outside advertising.

"Most agencies start from the perspective of doing a newspaper ad, or radio, outdoor, or TV. Those aren't our canvases," says Siltanen. "Our canvases are everything. Sometimes we tell clients that in the beginning they should not even be doing advertising. And they're kind of like, 'Whoa, aren't you an ad agency?' But that's not how advertising works! Maybe it used to work that way. But some aspects of this business, like looking at [problems] from a conventional standpoint, don't work that well anymore.

"From the outset, we decided we're going to come up with ideas which are so big and explosive, a client really doesn't have to pay for them. 'Toys' is a perfect example. How much is it worth to be named commercial of the year and be talked about in that way by *Rolling Stone* and *Time* and *Oprah*? That's free money to a client. And it's not just placement, either—it's making your product an issue to be discussed in detail by people every day versus a soda can that just happens to be sitting on the table and is just a can."

TEACHING CLIENTS NOT TO WANT THE WHOLE PIE

With one of the agency's first accounts—Freeinternet.com, a service that provided Internet access free in return for beaming advertising at its subscribers—the agency asked for a percentage of any other revenue streams its ideas created. "If it becomes a television show, if merchandise becomes something, we get a percentage of it," recalls Siltanen.

"If we turn a TV concept into a print concept, we get paid for doing the print ad. Why shouldn't we get paid when our idea is turned into a TV show, a toy, or key chain? I also told the client, most merchandising opportunities come through the agency. Shouldn't we have an incentive to pursue them? When I made this argument to Freeinternet.com, they said, 'You know what? It makes perfect sense.' "

Not every client has been so generous. Siltanen admits that the agency has had to be flexible and, in some cases, pass up nonadvertising rights to its properties. But he believes clients are misguided in wanting the whole pie. "This is an extension of the brand. The agency should be paid just like they do when they do a television spot. If we do a spot which is so good it leads to the creation of a television show, that's a great thing and everybody should win," he argues.

For Freeinternet.com, the agency created a character, Baby Bob, a little pitchbaby with a man's voice. It was an instant sensation. "The client's Web site was flooded," says Siltanen. "People were going crazy. We got a call from the head of Tri-Star and then from Viacom. We ended up doing a deal with Viacom which led to a show called *Baby Bob*, which became a hit prime-time show on CBS."

IT'S ALL ABOUT WHO'S GOING TO OWN THE INTELLECTUAL PROPERTY

Siltanen urges agencies that aspire to create intellectual property with a life beyond ads to make it very clear in the pitch stage that they believe they should have some rights to what is created. He believes that clients certainly have rights to the work they commission and to the ideas in the ads produced for them, but anything beyond that should be either deeded to the agency or shared.

"The model changes with every client," he says. "Some are willing to pay more for exclusivity and others are not. Also, it depends on whether we have already created a character prior to meeting them or if they're hiring me to create one. If they're hiring me only to create a character within a 'standard' advertising context, then that character should be theirs for those purposes. But when it's used for a movie or a television show, then we should talk about that."

Rob Siltanen's Approach to Intellectual Property

- Clients hire agencies to make ads. They want to own the rights to all the intellectual property created for an ad. If that's what the contract of hire says, then that's the law.
- If characters or original content are used outside the ad—in merchandising, entertainment, the branding of other products, or to advertise products in markets other than originally intended— then the agency should participate in that additional revenue.
- Agencies have to learn how to raise these issues in their original compensation conversations with clients.
- There is no rule of thumb for the fee these "new uses" should earn. But when talking about sharing revenues beyond advertising, both sides might start from the premise that devising a rights fee or commission should equate to what the client would have paid the agency if it had been hired to come up with original programming and not just advertising.
- Neither side needs to be greedy. This should be a win-win situation for both sides. It's in the interest of the client to get the icon into the mainstream of the culture, because every "free" mention of the icon rebounds to a higher profile for the brand. The more chihuahua toy dogs sold, the more people thought about Taco Bell.

IN THE FUTURE, YOU MAY GROW YOUR OWN IDEAS OR HIRE THEM

Meanwhile other companies are starting to move into the ad world's creative space. One, @radical.media, which started out as a

New York–based commercial production company and now has offices in Los Angeles, London, Paris, Berlin, and Sydney, doesn't see itself as a threat to traditionally oriented ad agencies but as an adjunct to them.

"The reason we changed the name of this company in 1994 [from Sandbank Kamen & Partners] was that we thought with all the changes in the media landscape and the proliferation and fragmentation of media, it was time to reconsider the 30-second TV commercial format as a way for a brand to create a relationship with a consumer," says @radical.media CEO Jonathan Kamen.

"For a long time no one in traditional advertising paid much attention to these changes. But gradually, a few agencies and clients have been warming up to them. Today, it's certainly more fashionable with the success of alternative marketing ideas like Fallon's BMW Films to talk about branded content. Now we get a steady, weekly flow of clients and agencies asking us to explore this frontier."

To Kamen, it's all a kind of a *Back to the Future* phenomenon. He recalls the days of the *General Electric Theater* on television and *The Borden Show* brought to you by Elsie the Cow—a time when it was natural for agencies to think up single-sponsor shows and provide their clients with opportunities to own content. "There was real appreciation for a brand to be bringing you something," he says. "But in order to think of branded content, you have to get your feet wet producing valuable content, period. So we have been experimenting with all kinds of projects."

Kamen doesn't want @radical.media to turn into a product placement firm. "Blatant product placement is not the approach I want us to take," he says. "I want to see the brand more logically integrated into the program. We did a one-hour special for Nike on the Winter Olympics using Charles Barkley as the narrator. There was no [indication] that Nike had sponsored the program. It didn't matter as long as they were supporting a premier athlete and creating more enthusiasm for the sport by having shared a little more knowledge of what athletes go through.

"That was a perfect example of brand-supported content versus branded content. I want to be proud of programming we're producing and see the brands we work with succeed. It's important for us to develop a template, an understanding of what the consumer appreciates. When sponsors started out producing their own programming, ads were pretty awful. They hit you over the head with the brand message. In the past 25 years, we have learned how to make some commercials far more entertaining than the programming itself. I want to ensure that we enrich the culture—not pollute it."

Along these lines, @radical.media recently produced a two-hour movie for ABC, *Report from Ground Zero,* involving interviews with firefighters talking about the September 11 tragedy, and for VH1, a documentary based on a book about Africa in the *Day in the Life . . .* series.

@radical.media has pushed so deeply into new turf that it was honored by *BusinessWeek* magazine recently as one of the nation's top seven design firms, along with Nike, Apple, and Frog Design. Recent design projects include helping Descente and Eiko Ishioua design the Winter Olympics uniforms for the Japanese, Swiss, Spanish, and Canadian teams and helping IBM create an installation at an amusement park in Orlando. "To me, being cited by *BusinessWeek* was a great moment of achievement for our diversification effort," says Kamen. "Our agency friends no longer look at us as just a production company."

Are agencies nervous about a production company becoming a content creator? Not really, says Kamen. "[Agencies] recognize they have certain abilities and strengths in terms of understanding of brands, and they've always outsourced production. It's not competition, but an extension of a natural partnership."

As to whether the company will find itself more often working directly with clients, Kamen answers the question obliquely: "We are looking for ways to collaborate intelligently with existing agencies," he says. "I don't think we have lost sight of the value a traditional agency brings to the party. Yet we're looking for agencies who have embraced the need to evolve as partners. That's our strength. We would prefer to work with agencies which understand the concept of marketing beyond traditional advertising."

WHAT IF WE COME FULL CIRCLE AND THE MEDIA BUYER IS THE POWER?

Or the model may grow from a new kind of planning-centric media company. Any independent media house comfortable with presenting *as the primary expenditure of a brand* nonprint and non-TV approaches is on its way to becoming such a resource. But the deciding factor will be its ability to read the consumer and the competitive set. If it has *in-house* strategic planning capabilities, then it can claim a readiness to determine brand strategy. It will be natural for clients to gradually entrust such companies with control of greater parts of their advertising and promotions budgets. It takes only one major success to win a client's trust.

From then on, the company will live off its ability to manage accounts. Most clients, at least in the United States, do not put their advertising budgets with agencies because of a particular creative team. They give agencies these assignments because of their ability to guide the brand. As such budgets become more fragmented, the senior media planner, given enough resources, will have as much opportunity to determine how the budget is spent as anyone else in the marketing mix.

It's only a short hop, skip, and jump from controlling a budget to entrusting a strategic media planner with the influence and even control of all the creative resources necessary to execute such plans. In the new era of cost-consciousness, it may be cheaper for a large unbundled media firm to hire freelancers or to go to smaller independent agencies like WONGDOODY and Modernista!, or even to @radical.media, to carry out such assignments rather than to commission a traditionally organized advertising agency. Such agencies suffer from higher costs and overheads. It isn't long before the support of too many lightly used resources (e.g., media buying, account planning, promotions) drives agency costs too high.

HOW CAN WE DESCRIBE THIS NEW KIND OF AGENCY?

Of course, some of the agencies that will define the future will be formed out of the shells of current agencies. Just because an agency continues to do traditional ads and commercials in a traditional manner doesn't prevent it from being a contender, but there will be certain sine qua nons to qualify for this elite list.

First, such agencies must be media-neutral and have an openness to unusual ideas. Let's start with how Graham Warsop approaches a problem in his award-winning South African agency, The Jupiter Drawing Room. The JDR has won more awards from Clio and Cannes in the past five years than many top British and American agencies with three or four times its billings. What's interesting is how Warsop doesn't stack the deck. According to him, the process starts when he calls in four or five creative teams and explains the challenge facing a client or prospect.

Warsop says his people are given four to seven days for the initial thinking. "It goes back to the way we structure the agency," says Warsop. "People around the table include specialists in new media, design, and relationship marketing as well as classical creative teams trained to think below the line. Obviously, the guidelines on budget and the strategic position of the brand are givens, but otherwise we don't limit thinking. People are encouraged to think laterally—anything is possible."

For a local music store chain, the agency devised a "karaoke kit"—a shower curtain with lyrics of popular songs plus a bar of soap in the shape of a microphone—which was sold as a promotion in the stores, but generated plenty of PR for the store. For KFM, a radio station that wanted to support a gun-free alliance, the agency adapted a vending machine to look as if it were dispensing guns. The machines were placed in shopping malls. The coin box acted as a collection box.

Any agency that still makes most of its revenue/profit from traditional ads certainly might be wary of morphing into a media-neutral idea house. Similarly, leadership will partly depend on the skill sets available inside the agency. A planning-based agency has more of a chance of advancing than one still relying on traditional, research-based analytic tools for interpreting consumer attitudes.

The other thing to remember is that a modern, integrated campaign needs to saturate the target with communications—and can leverage many very inexpensive kinds of media to extend the media budget. A good example of this kind of integrated saturation campaign can be seen in the work of Luckie & Co. in Birmingham, Alabama, whose campaign for Tobacco Free Families won a Media Lion at Cannes. The client wanted to persuade low-income, pregnant women in eight poverty-level counties to stop smoking. The agency, working with a limited budget on a hard-to-reach, cynical target, focused on the fact that a sick baby interferes with the mother's ability to be a wage earner.

The agency started by sending pregnant mothers a direct-mail (requested) "I can quit" kit. It then advertised the kit via lost-and-found posters in laundromats. It also put "Missing Healthy Baby" stickers on pay phones and around high-traffic grocery stores. Anyone buying a pregnancy test kit received a coupon that said, "Think you might be pregnant? If so, you need to quit smoking, and we can help," which included the telephone number of the Tobacco Free hotline. The coup de grâce was to borrow what appeared to be official government cars and to label them, "Department of Secondhand Smoke, Transportation Division." The cars, driven through poor neighborhoods, created the impression that it was against the law to smoke—a conclusion that, though untrue, helped increase anxiety about harming kids with secondhand smoke.

Intellectual capital will be more of a premium in the future. Agencies will need access to very sophisticated databases about consumer trends in order to be effective. They may come to clients with great ideas and great insights—but they will need some science to prove their ideas and make them work. Such agencies will have to become more adept at amassing the kind of data that Procter & Gamble and other sophisticated clients bring to a problem. The strategic insight may (and probably should) grow out of intuition, but it has to fit the data or in some way be planning-based in order to have a reasonable chance of success.

It won't be enough to understand which programs consumers watch and which magazines they read. Marketers will need to know how various media intersect with the consumer's core interests and how the media is consumed. All of this can be illuminated by research—qualitative and quantitative—but it will tip the scales toward larger companies with the resources to tap into this kind of proprietary understanding.

Agencies and marketers will gradually become comfortable with new media. If TiVo and such digital screens manage to block or narrow the reach of traditional TV commercials, agencies will have to learn how to overcome such barriers—perhaps by making their communications part of the content or, as BMW Films has shown, making it so entertaining that consumers seek it out.

Inserting a client's message or brand or product into a program can be accomplished through product placements, which suffer at times from being obvious and seemingly out of place, or through more subtle and better-fitting "sponsorships" of content, or even by creating the kind of content (e.g., @radical.media's Nike-commissioned walkup to the Tour de France) so valuable it is sought out by the consumer, regardless of origin.

Integration of the message will become even more important in this fragmented media environment. As a result, we will no doubt witness the evolution of a totally new kind of agency, one that will present itself as more of an integrator or brand steward and not necessarily as an ad agency at all. There are no doubt already pure integrators out there—small agencies and consultants that have been retained to act as a kind of external marketing department for a client.

This is the kind of role played by consultants with former client or agency credentials, like Sergio Zyman. Zyman, author of two books seeking to debunk traditional marketing methodology and formerly chief marketing officer of Coca-Cola, currently heads his own consulting agency, Zyman Marketing Group, whose clients include Chase Bank, Callaway Golf, and the Mexican government.[2] Zyman preaches that no matter how big the client's company, advertising has to have a single chief. "If you don't control exactly what you want communicated, your inaction or mistakes will do it for you," he writes in *The End of Advertising as We Know It*.

MAYBE THE FUTURE IS DEFINED MORE BY ATTITUDE THAN BY STRUCTURE

Those who have had the opportunity to consult with clients in these matters know of their openness to unusual approaches that promise a better return on the marketing and advertising investment. Clients more than ever are ready to experiment with new business models if they can be assured of more impact. They have gone to agencies because they thought what they needed was an ad. Now they know better: They need to *build brands*; they need to *sell products*. If ads can do this most effectively, then fine, they need more ads. But if sponsoring Lance Armstrong inspires employees to have more enthusiasm for their work and does a better job of polishing the image of the U.S. Postal Service, then maybe the $10 to $20 million a year spent on the USPS bicycle team offers a much better return than an equivalent amount of TV commercial time.

Brands are emotional things that exist largely in the minds of consumers. It's not enough just to make a product. You eventually have to touch the consumer in a variety of ways—one of them being communications.

Brands communicate through the packaging, through what others say about the brand, through the experience the consumer has when buying the product and using it—as well as in the more deliberate forms of communication such as advertising, direct mail, promotions, public relations, and so on.

Agencies have traditionally owned the advertising space. It is their business and their art to lose. Others huddling round the marketplace are eager to supplant agencies now that they are having difficulty transforming their services to the new, fragmented spectrum of media and the new consumer. The game is by no means over.

Agencies that learn how to embrace new media and how to help brands in this new media universe will be assured a bright future. It's probably helpful for such agencies to change the focus of their work. Instead of dedicating themselves to producing great advertising, they should take a pledge to produce powerful, business-building ideas. This gives them a broader mission and ensures their relevance in the new frontier.

This is not just a linguistic trick. Once you have adopted a media-neutral, idea-centered approach to communication, everything in your company and its processes must change. Change, if approached correctly, is a great tonic.

The future suddenly becomes very bright indeed. You start landing fish left and right, and you're assured of going home with what fishing writer Roger Menard calls "a full creel."

THE LAST WORD . . . FROM A FISHERMAN, OF COURSE

In preparing this book, I've enjoyed rereading not only many of the advertising titles in our den, but also the small library of fly-fishing texts I've collected over the years. The thought I'd like to conclude this study with is this: While the future for agencies might be somewhat clouded, the premium that clients are ready to put on *ideas* should actually serve as an inspiration for young people entering the advertising business.

Advertising is, after all, not quite the same as other high-profile business disciplines such as investment banking, engineering, or consulting. It is much more a mixture of commerce and art. Therefore, as Mike Donahue of the American Association of Advertising Agencies notes, it should attract a different kind of person than those who gravitate to Wall Street or to the nation's great consulting houses— not only someone with imagination, but with a love of the hunt, whatever the difficulties. Helping a brand grow is really a very exciting, rewarding experience.

Permit me to end this book with a quotation from one of my favorite fly-fishing books, *My Side of the River*, by Roger Menard, a conservationist who hangs out in upstate New York along the Esopus River and who is a member of the Catskill Fly Tyers Guild and Museum, charter director of the Theodore Gordon Flyfishers, and a member of Trout Unlimited.

Writes Menard: "Anglers spend a lifetime wading rivers, making plans, and devising all sorts of techniques to place a fly in the corner of a fish's mouth. If the fisherman takes angling seriously, he is usually rewarded, and in the process becomes proficient at his craft. As the years pass, aggressiveness begins to wane and a sense of satisfaction is derived purely from being at the river's edge. Enjoyment of the sport branches out far beyond what occurs beneath the water's surface."[3]

Making advertising is a lot of fun. Being sure your advertising or whatever you do for a client is driven by good ideas is, in my way of thinking, much more rewarding. Keep fishing for ideas and you should develop a rich and deep sense of satisfaction, which, to rephrase Menard's evocative words, branches out far beyond what occurs beneath the market's surface.

LEADERSHIP LESSONS FOR BECOMING THE AGENCY OF THE FUTURE

✔ Reform your agency—from your mission statement to how you arrange the desks to the titles you give your people—on an idea-centric model, not an advertising model.

✔ Anything that does not lead to providing great, business-transforming ideas should be discarded or reworked.

✔ Become truly media-neutral by ensuring that you are paid roughly the same fees for nonadvertising ideas as for advertising ideas.

✔ Be prepared to operate in an unbundled marketplace, where every service—even down to and including the integration of communications—may be farmed out. Ask yourself which of your services can reasonably be considered best of class. Anything that doesn't measure up—stop offering. Fix it or shut it down.

✔ Listen to the marketplace. If clients want ideas based on planning, then add planning to the mix. If they want strategy, either start providing it or find someone who does. If they just want ads, then give them the best ads in the world. But don't let them get away calling you just a manufacturer of ads. Ads are ideas, too.

✔ Look at how you are paid. If you provide a premium service, then maybe that's worth a premium price.

✔ Take a fresh look at how you talk to clients about the intellectual property you create. Stop amortizing ideas over five years. Make clients pay you a fair price for your work each year—and when they want ideas that go beyond advertising, discuss with them other forms of compensation.

APPENDIX A

Advertising's Invisible Values

MARTIN SORRELL, GROUP CHIEF EXECUTIVE, WPP GROUP PLC[1]

This subject you're addressing this week [client compensation] is a hugely important one. It's important for everybody. For clients and agencies; for management and staff; for consumers and for share-owners.

My only criticism is with your timing. This conference, in my view, would have been more valuable had it been held earlier. Much earlier. About a 150 years earlier, in fact.

How many other multi-billion-dollar industries can you think of who'd wait 150 years or so before trying to work out what it was they provided, why it was of value to their customers, and how much they deserved to get paid for it?

I may be being a little harsh on us for saying that. But looking at our conference program for the next two days, it's clear that at the heart of it all—certainly at the *start* of it all—lies the need to ask and answer exactly those questions.

Everyone of us here, I suppose, would welcome a more rational set of compensation criteria: so long, of course, as more rational didn't mean less income. But how can we expect to make more sense of our pricing policy when we remain so vague and so inarticulate about what it is that we sell?

I hope this conference will do many things. I hope we will remind ourselves of the commercial value to clients of the simple act of advertising; of what agencies can do to increase the value of the time and space that clients buy; and of some of the less obvious benefits that the advertising development process brings with it.

And to encourage you along these lines, let me start by telling you—however familiar with the story you may be—something about the frozen lasagne market in the United Kingdom.

Until about five years ago, there were three frozen lasagnas on the market in Britain, and they were all reasonably successful. Each had its own advertising campaign; and each advertising campaign pointed out quite skillfully just why this particular frozen lasagne differed from, and was superior to, the others. Then along came a fourth frozen lasagne which decided to do something completely different.

They'd done some sensitive consumer research—and discovered that their competitors had been so preoccupied with pointing up their fairly negligible differences that nobody had reminded consumers of the glory and satisfactions of frozen lasagne as a category.

And that, courageously, is what the fourth brand decided to do. In their advertising, they showed very engagingly just why frozen lasagne as such met the needs of the modern fragmented family—a point that could have been made equally well by any of their competitors. As a result, this fourth brand of lasagne increased its sales by a certified 180% and stopped being the fourth brand and became the first brand instead. And furthermore, the total market for frozen lasagne grew greatly.

I hope you don't mind being compared to frozen lasagne. And I hope you see the point. I have often thought that advertising agencies become so preoccupied with pointing up their often negligible differences that we forget to remind clients and others of the glories and satisfactions of advertising and agencies *as a category*.

Because of my relatively late arrival on the scene—and because I observe obsessively rather than actually practice the trade—I may have a combination of ignorance and interest that allows me to say a few things about the agency business that some of you could not; and I hope to take advantage of your invitation today to do exactly that.

And I hope that, if we become just a little clearer about what it is we do—what it is we sell—exactly what it is that we contribute to our clients' prosperity, then it may also lead to a more rational and equitable approach to compensation and reward. (But that, of course, is the easy bit—which is why I intend to leave it up to you.)

I plan to look at three overlapping areas of agency contribution this afternoon. The first is extremely obvious; the second is almost as obvious but harder to define; and the third is the one that intrigues me most because it has no name, is never paid for—yet is often the most valuable of them all.

So first, the most obvious; and the most obvious victim of the frozen lasagne effect.

To most clients, in most competitive markets, the most important decision about advertising is the decision to advertise in the first place. With what agency? Yes, of course that matters. With which campaign? Yes, of course, often critical. But neither question is as fundamental as the first.

The very fact of advertising begins to make goods and services famous; begins to give them familiarity and a reassuring sense of reliability; is the beginning of the establishment of a brand personality and brand values.

Just pulling up the name on some billboards may not be very sophisticated . . . it may not be very creative . . . and it does little to promote one agency's abilities in comparison with another's—but for the client, it's a great deal better than doing nothing; it's the all-important beginning of consumer marketing.

In agencies, we know all that—and we think everybody else does too. So we concentrate in our competitive way on the extra value we can offer clients—through better media buying and better creative work.

It really is in most clients' interests to maintain their advertising presence. But will they all do it, I wonder, if nobody reminds them of the commercial rewards of doing so and the commercial penalties of not doing so? Because what they tend to be told, of course, as they go from one agency presentation to another, is that as long as they do the sensible thing and switch their account to us, they can achieve the same marketing objectives with far fewer dollars.

I believe that more agencies should be more ready to make the simple point about the fundamental value of advertising at all. We may think that it weakens our case—that it somehow diminishes our importance if we admit that, even at our best, we can only contribute 10 to 20 cents' worth to every advertising dollar spent. In fact, to my mind, by putting the realistic case, we strengthen rather than weaken our argument—while simultaneously reinforcing the fundamental case for advertising in the first place.

To some extent, I believe, we're still inhibited by the paradox of the commission effect.

In theory, as every client has from time to time pointed out, the commission system should have encouraged agencies to put the case to clients for maintaining and increasing their advertising expenditure: constantly, compellingly perhaps even to the point of tedium. But in practice, so sensitive are agencies to accusations of self-interest—that they seem to flinch whenever the subject of money is raised. (This may, for the record, be the only occasion on which advertising agency people have been publicly credited with sensitivity.)

My next point concerns the hugely difficult area of The Big Idea.

I suppose it must be [about 65] years ago . . . that Leo Burnett—probably in person—first presented his client, the Minnesota Valley Canning Company, with some early, sketchy thoughts for a character to be called the Jolly Green Giant.

Nobody in 1935 could have known just how good an idea that was. Nobody, in fact, *at that time*, could have been absolutely certain that it was a good idea at all. And I doubt if anybody to this day could put a dollar value on that idea—and hope to get to within a few billion or so.

But there are some certainties. It was an idea which immediately set the canning company's products apart from the competition. It gave the company stability and personality. It demonstrated protected profit margins in sectors which were otherwise doomed to become commodities. It facilitated new brand launches and extensions. It proved as successful outside the United States as within. And it's 60 years old and still going strong.

And the final certainty is this: No kind of organization *other than a marketing-based advertising agency* could have come up with that idea.

To an outsider, it may not seem such an amazing idea at all: What's so clever about calling something "The Jolly Green Giant?" Surely anybody could have thought of that.

And so they could. But the point, of course, is that they wouldn't. Because only if you know what you're looking for—and *why* you're looking for it—will an idea be relevant.

There's the famous story of the English painter Whistler—taken to court by a disgruntled client who claimed that Whistler had grossly overcharged him for a simple pencil sketch. Thinking he was making the crucial, damning point, the client's lawyer leaned forward and said: "So tell me, Mr. Whistler, just how long did it take to complete this work?"

And Whistler replied: "A lifetime, sir."

How long did it take Leo Burnett to think of the Jolly Green Giant in 1935? I don't know—probably 10 minutes. But also, of course, a lifetime. Because only a creative agency with real experience of markets and consumers and communications could have used that 10 minutes so relevantly and so profitably.

I asked Burt Manning [then CEO of J. Walter Thompson] for an instant, top-of-the-head list of other profit-making advertising ideas—from anywhere, not just Thompson. These are some of his candidates:

- Have you driven a Ford lately?
- Good Food and Good Ideas from Kraft
- Marlboro Country
- The Pepsi Generation
- Nike's "Just Do It"
- Do Blondes Have More Fun?
- The Kodak Moment
- "Do you know me?" from American Express
- When You're Out of Schlitz, You're Out of Beer

All strong brand ideas. All of huge and immeasurable commercial value to their owners. All created by agencies who contributed both strategic thinking and creativity to their clients' businesses.

Burt went on to make this further point: Almost all those long-term, profit-building ideas were created before the real squeeze on agency compensation which began in the early '80s. Since then, in many agencies, investment in strategic and creative resources has gone into decline. And to use Burt's words, "The great brand- and profit-building campaigns have been few and far between."

If he's right—and I suspect he is—then the agency business as a whole has some serious work to do. And clients, if they're thoughtful clients, will—in their own self-interest—actively encourage us to do it.

Forgive me for making this point so repeatedly, but it does get forgotten. Big ideas, like people, need two parents each. Big ideas are only big ideas if born of analysis, hard graft and experience—as well as creative inspiration.

A few weeks ago, Charlotte Beers [then chairman of Ogilvy & Mather, another WPP company] published Ogilvy & Mather's declaration of Shared Values. One paragraph reads: "We prize both analytical and creative skills. Without the first, you can't know where to go; without the second, you won't be able to get there." And it's precisely that combination that makes the generation of relevant, profit-making ideas most likely.

None of this solves the problem of how such ideas might be paid for, of course—at least, not directly. What was the Jolly Green Giant worth? How might he have been paid for? In advance? As a rolling royalty? In retrospect? Almost certainly, in none of these ways.

But if the process is understood, then the value of marketing a constant agency culture may also be understood.

You can't expect to buy great ideas on a one-off basis—and then stand everybody down 'til they're needed again. Great ideas will only emerge from deep and constant immersion in the client's markets. And that, I would suggest, is what the client should be asked to pay for: not the ideas themselves. But all that, as I mentioned earlier, is for you, not me, to decide—before tomorrow evening [when the conference ends]—and I much look forward to hearing your solutions.

Of all the values an agency can have for a client, the last of my three may be easily the most valuable—but is certainly the least visible. Furthermore, unlike my first two, a large part of the value will be enjoyed by the client whether or not he decides to use advertising at all.

Just about the only assertion that management gurus would agree on, I suspect, would go something like this: The closer a company is to its ultimate consumers . . . the more it understands them . . . the more sensitively it interprets what those consumers say and do . . . then the more likely that company is to be successful—and remain successful.

Now, sensitivity to consumers is not shared equally among all kinds of business. And my belief is this: that if you took very broad categories of enterprise, from all around the world, and then arranged them into a sort of hierarchy of consumer sensitivity, you'd end up with something like this:

Right at the bottom, at the least sensitive end of the scale (and ignoring national governments) you would get state-run utilities. Then heavy industry. Then business-to-business. Then consumer financial services. Then high-ticket consumer goods. And at the top of the heap, obviously with some exceptions, but in general well ahead in the understanding of their markets, would come the repeat-purchase, low-ticket, everyday consumer goods companies.

And if you then took each of those categories and listed what each of them spent, on a pro rata basis, on consumer advertising, you would find an almost exact match in terms of relativity: with those at the bottom, at the insensitive end, spending little or nothing—and those at the top spending a lot.

Put as starkly as that, of course, it sounds as if I'm about to argue that the very act of advertising makes companies more efficient—and that would be ridiculous.

My real point is this: The decision to advertise—and to advertise thoughtfully—carries with it a great many other implications. Properly executed, the advertising development process is like a long and often hazardous voyage of discovery. What do people think of the brand and the company? What do they think of its competitors? How would they respond to this message, this change of position, this appeal?

When focus groups and other research techniques are properly used, real people are invited to respond to real things in a way that never happens in any other form of strategic development. You unearth people's knowledge . . . ignorance . . . fears . . . prejudices . . . and aspirations. You discover what they really think of you . . . and your company.

Identifying strategy is as creative a task as inventing the ads at the end of it all. It involves logic and flair; analysis and guesswork; trial and error. It involves getting things wrong and putting them right again . . . and listening to people and knowing when to take notice and when to ignore. It involves perseverance and experience and professional confidence.

And surprisingly, often at the end of that process—and long before a single advertisement has run—the client company will be in possession of something beyond price: the clearest picture they will ever have looked at of themselves and their competitors; and through the only eyes that matter, the eyes of their consumers.

Everyone in this room will know of examples where the communications development process will have revealed to major companies not just new advertising appeals, but new trading positions and even new corporate strategies, involving modified products and new priorities.

All this can happen, of course, only if top management wants it to happen, wants to be part of it, and is determined to make use of it.

There are still some companies—though mostly, I have to say, at the bottom of my notional pyramid—who believe that marketing is done by the marketing department and that advertising has nothing to do with corporate strategy. But the good companies know better. They know that the endless stream of insight and guidance that springs from the development process must reach top management; because if it stops with the advertising people, then only the communications will be modified and the real and priceless value of that knowledge will be wasted.

There's been recent evidence of this in the financial services market—particularly, I think, in the UK.

When financial services companies first began to advertise, they failed to modify their products and their language: they behaved as if "marketing" was just something you bolted on at the end of the manufacturing process. As a result, many consumers were baffled by the complexity and remoteness of much of what was now on offer.

But now, increasingly, these same companies are building their business strategies from the outside in. They're learning how to position themselves in ways which make sense not just to brokers and other financial institutions, but to the ultimate consumer. And they've been guided in these ways, sometimes quite dramatically, by the clues, the insights, and the revelations that have come to them as a direct result of the decision to advertise.

Around the world, at conferences such as this, agencies are asking themselves if their relationship with clients has become less important. If they've increasingly become suppliers of advertisements rather than strategic advisers: In other words, if they've allowed themselves to drift downstream.

And allied to this is the question: Are the consultancies poised to take over? If the agencies have left an upstream vacuum, won't the management and marketing consultants be only too pleased to fill it? And this second question is usually followed by cries of how unfair and unjust it will be if these ignorant outsiders end up being paid vast sums of money for doing something a good deal less effectively than we used to do for absolutely nothing.

As you might imagine, I share that concern. And I very much hope that this conference addresses it. I remain absolutely of the opinion that only an organization such as a full-service advertising agency, containing as it does both the analytical and the creative skills, can provide client companies with the truly sensitive insights they need to build, nourish, and reposition their brands. In other words, to remain competitive.

But not all clients think that, and it's not surprising. We can hardly blame them for failing to value a service which we've never given a name to, and never asked them to pay for.

In the days when the commission system ruled unchallenged, maybe it didn't matter that much. But with agency compensation, under scrutiny everywhere, and agency management looking to contain costs wherever they can, there seems to be a very serious risk indeed that—if advertising's invisible values continue to be invisible—they will simply cease to be.

APPENDIX B

A Big Future for Big Ideas

MT Rainey, CEO, Rainey Kelly Campbell Roalfe/Y&R[1]

The status of our industry is colored by the overwhelming impression of mediocrity it creates in our culture. But it is saved by the beacons that occasionally penetrate this carapace of cliché to publicly transform brands and businesses.

It's my belief that our industry is facing both its biggest challenge and its biggest opportunity ever at this time.

The challenge is to significantly raise the status of the industry and restore clients' confidence in the effectiveness and indispensability of advertising per se and the opportunity to establish primacy in the ability to deliver that most valuable of competitive weapons—in fact some would say *the last real competitive weapon*—creativity and ideas.

The former is a defense of advertising if you like and I believe that needs to be made, and the latter is a mandate for agencies to change and to refocus on a new definition of creativity that repositions and reestablishes agencies as key strategic partners with clients in managing brands.

To me, the issue at the heart of both the challenge *and* the opportunity revolves round the concept of *the idea.* I am passionate about the belief that ideas are the key competitive weapon in business today. As brands are the engine of business, so ideas are the rocket fuel of brands.

A lot of rhetoric at the moment would have us believe that for clients integration is Job One. Well to me integration is like fresh air—what I think you in America call Motherhood and what we in Britain tend to call The Bleeding Obvious. Of course, integration is a good thing and clients should want to get more of it—but I think that as more and more clients acknowledge and see the benefits of an integrated message, more and more of them are realizing that the biggest challenge they face in achieving real benefits from it is not in who does it or how it gets done or how to get a one-stop shop or how to get agencies to work better together. But in finding a powerful, motivating and differentiating idea to integrate around.

I believe the idea is Job One.

But what do we mean by the idea when we talk about it this way? Well "idea" is a word that agencies have always overused and have therefore undervalued. The idea isn't to use a particular celebrity or a certain soundtrack or a particular graphic or photographic look; nor an end line; or a technique or a storyline though all these things may be vital to the execution. Yet many people in advertising still identify these types of things as the idea.

An idea is neither strategy nor execution but something between the two and bigger and more valuable than both. A single creative or intellectual property that clearly and consistently communicates something *about the brand*.

The idea is the bit that sticks to the brand after we've seen the ads; the idea is the thing we perceive about the brand through the ads.

And perhaps more importantly than that, the idea can be communicated in any form in any medium. An idea transcends execution and is inherently repeatable. It lives at the level of the brand—and should be able to be brought to life in all of its communications.

The idea is the center of gravity of a brand's marketing. Of course, it cannot therefore be an exclusive property of the advertising or be advertising dependent.

I believe ideas are the most valuable things agencies have always provided and certainly the most valuable things they could provide in an integrated future where advertising per se may not be the center of the client's universe.

But the systems, structure, and practices of agencies do not mandate the identification or provision of an idea, far less agreement to it between interested parties. The idea is mostly a by-product of the advertising, and most worryingly, very often there is no idea at all—nothing that sticks to the brand in a way that is memorable and meaningful.

"The client bought the idea" is a familiar mantra of agency people—yet clients have never bought ideas. We have never asked them to—we've never put a price on them. Which is part of the problem. In fact, as the chairman of a top five U.S. agency said at a conference recently: "We were basically a TV production house. It was all systems go to capture that lucrative 15% revenue stream. Thinking, research, strategy, creativity—that was a free gift to our clients. Like Super Bowl tickets. Now we don't know how to make money."

To paraphrase JFK, the enemy of the truth is not a lie, it is the myth. Pervasive, plausible and popular. One of the biggest myths in our industry is that advertising is a creative business. We in advertising certainly like to think of ourselves as being in a creative business. But this is far from being true. We may be engaged in a creative *endeavor* but we are not in the business of creativity.

Our business—that is, "the basis on which we make money"—is still related to and correlated with the volume production of ads and the volume of media expenditure in making and showing them. And while recent surveys certainly indicate that this is changing, it's still true that the majority of agency income is still derived from a formula based on client expenditures, whether it is paid in commissions or in pre-agreed monthly fees.

So, while classical commission payments are certainly less fashionable, the commission culture continues to both underlie and undermine our client relationships and the standing of our industry in the eyes of business leaders. We continue to be paid solely for outputs and not for inputs.

Insidiously, the commission system effectively removed pricing from the agency competitive equation, thereby reducing agencies to commodities and ignoring the value of the very thing the client was shopping for in the first place—a better product; a better relationship; a better idea.

The legacy that we live with, and the root cause of many of the problems in our industry is this: creative thinking, our best and most valuable product—our "free thinking"—is precisely that. *Free*. We've been giving it away for nothing.

Another myth about advertising is that it is a fast moving and innovative business. Fast moving, certainly. But innovative on it's own behalf, certainly not. Advertising is one of the most conservative businesses on this planet.

And advertising isn't changing. *It is being changed*, by the threat of management and branding consultants moving in our "upstream" territory. By the total emancipation of media planning and buying from the agency skill set. By the nature and fragmentation of media itself. And perhaps most importantly, by an increasing and quite proper client focus on brand ideas that go beyond advertising solutions—to say nothing of the willingness of other kinds of companies to attempt to provide them.

Can we be surprised that clients do not value from us what we have traditionally not asked them to value or pay for? And can we be surprised that others can step into that breach, ready to charge handsomely for what we have given away for free—because they can see its value?

What this new reality means is that the black box of what an agency actually does is effectively exposed and the advertising industry is being forced to consider what its core competencies really are: how it creates value; how it makes money; and what business it is really in.

We are now quite rightly being compelled to ask for recognition and compensation for what we have traditionally given away for free. The corollary of this is that we have to let go of an income culture that marks up volume, either in media or production terms, since we neither manufacture commercials nor buy media.

The reality is that strategically informed creativity, resulting in communications "ideas" for the brand which forms the center of gravity of a client's marketing program, must be a core deliverable of today's agency and we must find a way to value and price it.

This is the premise on which we founded our agency in the early '90s—that we would focus on providing these ideas and that we would charge for them and profit by them as—and when—and if we did provide them. The corollary was that we would not profit from any margins or mark-ups on expenditures on their behalf. We would seek simply to break even on the service aspects of the business.

We created a company with radically restructured processes for achieving this as well as a very different remuneration and income platform, which reflected it. This certainly didn't give us nor did we claim any monopoly on ideas. Far from it. But at least we were practicing what we preached. Our agency brand had an idea and that idea made it distinctive and interesting.

The reason why ideas are more important than ever is because in these days of increasingly commoditized markets, creativity and innovation in strategies, ideas are more important than ever in providing the competitive edge between brands and products.

An idea can piercingly position a product or elegantly alienate its competition.

It can speak to the target market in a voice they haven't heard before.

An idea can force reappraisal of the brand or company.

Or it can make you think about a product or a category of products in a way you never have before.

An idea will create intangible value for a brand and company— and increasingly the value of intangibles is being counted and recognized by the stock market.

But to be recognized as prime suppliers of ideas requires us to acknowledge the distinction between craft creativity and conceptual creativity—or *creative thinking* about brands, markets and consumers. What we might call the creative work behind the creative work.

It requires us to seek, identify and glorify the ideas, and not simply worship "the ad." It requires us to construct our companies and our cultures around what the late great Jay Chiat always believed—that creative is not a department.

We use the word *creativity* to exclusively describe the back end of the process and we exclusively ascribe it to the dominion of a few individuals in the agency. This is not to suggest that craft or executional creativity is not vital and valuable or not highly specialized, but just that this definition of creativity, which confines itself to the craft skills of advertising, not only radically misrepresents and undervalues the front end of the process but it also compounds the perception that as an industry our creativity is advertising dependent. That we can't think more broadly, more conceptually, and therefore more usefully about our client's businesses.

The best creative people are often also great conceptual thinkers about markets and brands—in fact they almost always are. But so are the best account people and the best planners. The core skills required for ideas are ones that we the agencies already have in spades: strategic problem solving; inspired hypothesis testing; lateral thinking about brands, markets and customers; and creative thinking that includes but is not restricted to the craft skills of the TV commercial and the press ad.

If we recognize this, then I think that advertising agencies with the same skill set but a broader mindset could undergo a renaissance in the next 10 years—and it should be a renaissance of quality and the recognition of quality, a renaissance of creativity, and a renaissance of reputation.

In today's media-fragmented, consumer-controlled media world, I think our unique skills in differentiating brands for emotional, intangible reasons will be at a premium.

I think our ability to use communication to make brands visible, sexy, and attractive will be very much in demand. And of course we have to find more and better ways to more rigorously account for the contribution we make, but accountability is not an end in itself. Value creation is.

Which leads me to a defense of advertising per se. Well, somebody's got to do it. And apologies to our colleagues in design and interactive and anyone else here who's not in advertising—but people are always trying to write off advertising and it's very annoying for those of us who are realistic enough to know it's got to change, to know that it's never going to anyway.

Ten years ago everyone was writing off advertising and advertising agencies because of the inevitability of the 1-to-1 future—the power of direct marketing, the ability to reach people personally and privately with customized messages. Just five years ago, everyone was writing off advertising and advertising agencies as obsolete and irrelevant in a multimedia digital world in which consumers have access to perfect information through the Web and who would easily be able to avoid advertising in interactive digital media in which consumers are in control of their own media menus. Now they're writing off the industry because, at least here in the United States, the economy has really tumbled and advertising has been cut back to such an extent that it is doubtful whether it will ever recover.

I don't know about you, but I'm tired of hearing that sad old quote attributed to Lord Leverhulme that half my advertising works, but I just don't know which half. Well, fair enough—but if we want to talk about percentages, let's talk about the three percent of direct marketing that works.

But let's consider how brands will work in the new media environment which is a reality. It will grow and the Internet marketing business will come back and more and more people will go online and media will be more and more digital.

If consumers have all the power and all the choices at their fingertips—where they can potentially access "perfect information" about any company or product, then surely they will go looking for brands they know. Surely the role of the brand becomes even more important than ever. After all, brands came into being in the first place precisely to provide shortcuts to meaning in an increasingly complex world—guarantees of consistent quality in the brave new world of consumerism.

Marketing in the digital world will be about consumers seeking out brands they have already chosen in some way. Brands with which they already feel some affinity or attraction. Brands that are familiar to them and are known to be familiar to others like them. They're not going to compare the availability in silver of every model of car—just the BMW or the Range Rover that they've already set their heart on.

Put simply, they will not seek a deeper, more meaningful relationship with a brand they don't fancy in the first place.

And arguably, brand advertising will actually have to contain much less "information" than it does now because there will be cheaper and easier ways of carrying that information than TV, print or posters. Information about price, pack sizes, food values, ingredients, special promotions, and the environmental and employment practices of its manufacturer will be available to interested parties online.

So, I think, the convergence of digital TV and online computing could displace a huge part of the communications industry—but I think direct mail is under the biggest threat (I mean as distinct from direct marketing, which of course will thrive online).

So in this hugely complex world where perfect information is available, we will move from the model of the brand as a magnet— which was the model in the analog media world—to the model of the brand as a beacon, which is the model for the brand in the digital world—brighter, more visible, more alluring, and more accessible than other brands around it.

Brands will not shout, they will shine. In the new media age, when we are drowning in information and searching for meaning, the most valuable resources will be a point of view; the brightest beacon will be the visionary company, the principled company, and the company that stands for something as opposed to the company that reflects everything and stands for nothing.

And there will be no better, no more powerful, and no more cost-effective way to establish and build those kind of intangibles than brand advertising that captures attention and wins empathy.

And, if anything, this new media world will intensify the needs for brands to be built in a public arena. Adam Smith said that, for the most part, the function of wealth is the display of wealth. So it is with brands. Their function is display. People depend on other people recognizing what their brand choices say about them.

Brand building depends on a shared media experience. And that's why I'm so bullish on the future brand image advertising in conventional broadcast, above-the-line, mass media.

The Internet can help people buy things. It can help people choose things. But it can't make people want things. Or at least it will be an incredibly slow and inefficient way of making people want things. A weak builder of brand empathy, brand personality, and brand point of view.

The skills of advertising agencies to create and communicate intangibles of shared and recognizable values will be very much in demand. Brands need big ideas, but in turn agencies will need to move their creativity to a higher level, to the level of ideas that go above and beyond advertising, though certainly which include it.

So a redefinition of creativity to include upstream creative thinking and the delivery of brand ideas is not to deny the importance of advertising and the craft skill of making great ads. It is simply to broaden the scope of our industry to be recognized and rewarded for what we do. Which is to create something that wasn't there before. To add value to brands through intangibles that have disproportionate value, and to create properties and territories for clients which, unlike almost all the other assets they have, cannot be easily copied or dispatched.

We all have to find a way in our companies and with our clients to foster and promote this culture of conceptual creativity and creative thinking. Because of the necessity for certainty and predictability increasingly demanded by clients, the processes of large companies tend to mitigate against creativity. Having to be right at every stage makes creativity virtually impossible. *Companies in which failure is an option are likely to be the same companies in which success is a certainty.* Controversial I know, but there you are. Enlightened trial and error beats the planning of flawless intellectuals every time—we fail faster to succeed sooner.

So we have to build a culture in our companies and with our clients in which confidence and conviction, not certainty, is required. In which ideas are judged as well as measured, but in which creativity at every stage is an imperative, not an option. In which everyone approaches the problem from the "what if" or the "why not" instead of the "what is" and the "here's why not." In which the idea is the most elusive, most valued and most cherished prize of all and in which, when recognized and identified—a big part of the skill, by the way—is treated like the rare, endangered species that it is.

APPENDIX C

The IDEO Difference

CATHERINE FREDMAN[1]

You may not know IDEO's name, but the 24-year-old design firm is credited with envisioning and implementing a staggering list of products and services in a wide variety of fields. The Palo Alto, California, company's impact on the world of product innovation is akin to Tiger Woods's success in professional golf and Microsoft's clout in personal computing.

Its creations range from the first commercial mouse (for Apple Computer) to the innovative GriD laptop computer, from the first standup toothpaste tube (for Procter & Gamble's Crest) to the first robotic whale (for the movie *Free Willy*). Add to that list portable defibrillators, self-sealing sports water bottles, the Palm V organizer, and Oral-B's Squish Grip children's toothbrush.

As the company has moved into the creation of services and consumer experiences, IDEO has designed the patient-friendly DePaul Health Center emergency room in St. Louis, Missouri, worked with famed architect Rem Koolhaas for the Office for Metropolitan Architecture (OMA) to create the invisible technology at the innovative Prada "epicenter" facility in New York City, and even helped McDonald's cut in half the number of steps in its "Made for You" food-service process (while inventing a toaster that browns buns in 15 seconds).

This summer, when *BusinessWeek* published its acclaimed Industrial Design Excellence Awards (IDEAs), the design firm blew away the competition with a total of 14 awards. The publication termed

IDEO's achievement "astonishing." But what is truly astonishing is that these honors have extended a 10-year winning streak totaling 58 awards—almost double that of the nearest competitor.

Companies like McDonald's, Pepsi-Cola, and Steelcase International come to IDEO for advice because of the design firm's unique approach to innovation. "But," says IDEO President Tim Brown, "until innovation reaches the marketplace, it's of no value to business. We put things out into the world." Adds Steelcase CEO Jim Hackett, one of many admirers: "IDEO can take raw ideas from concept to marketing faster than any other company I've seen."

Essentially, IDEO is a creativity factory. About 350 people working in a network of offices stretching from San Francisco to London to Tokyo pump out more than 100 new products each year. The firm helped design Polaroid's I-Zone instant camera, the interiors of Amtrak's Acela high-speed trains that run between Washington, D.C. and Boston, and Steelcase's Work/Life Center in New York City, an interactive theme park and exhibition hall of office furniture and work settings.

General manager Tom Kelley describes the process that generates, identifies, and implements appropriate ideas in his best-selling book, *The Art of Innovation*. But, he's quick to say, "The magic is not in the steps of the 'what'; it's over in the 'how.' If 'what' is the methodology, then 'how' is work practices."

Take one of the first and most important steps in the process: understanding and observing. One of the favorite sayings at IDEO is "Innovation begins with an eye." The firm tends to see things differently because it literally sees different things than what focus groups and other conventional forms of market research typically turn up.

"The popular notions of the last decade were for companies to become customer-centered," says Steelcase"s Hackett. "Theories abounded that if you paid attention to what your customer wanted, you couldn't go wrong. But the truth is that customers often ask you to do wrong things, not because they're difficult to deal with but because they just don't know better. The distinction is moving from customer-focused to user-centered, and the ability to understand the users of their products is a cultural shift that corporations have to make."

Being user-centered is a skill IDEO hones by employing teams of experts in human factors—anthropology, ethnography, psychology—to observe how people actually use a product or approach a problem, whether it's a diabetic taking a daily dose of insulin, a work team huddled around a flip chart, or a person buying a can of Pepsi.

Recently, Pepsi called IDEO in to take a fresh look at vending. "We came at it from an operational standpoint: What can we manufacture?" recalls Megan Pryor, vice president of innovation at Pepsi-Cola. "They came at it from: What do consumers want from a vending machine? They spent hours watching people interact with vending machines. Consumers would never have verbalized, "I want bigger buttons," "I want to see my product," or "I don't want to reach into that dark hole in the bottom and not know what's down there." IDEO's method is good for figuring out what consumers want when they don't know what they want."

"IDEO does a remarkable job of taking observations and turning them into opportunities and eventually, innovations," Pryor concludes. "It takes packages that have existed for decades and gives them new life through improved functionality."

Observations get turned into ideas that can lead to innovations at brainstorming sessions. Brainstorming is practically a religion at IDEO; Kelley calls it "the idea engine" of the company's culture. These sessions are where IDEO's creativity is most evident, but they're also a manifestation of what can be achieved with the right methodology. The firm puts into practice Nobel Prize–winner Linus Pauling's oft-quoted belief that "The best way to get a good idea is to get a lot of ideas."

It's not uncommon for a 60-minute brainstormer to yield more than 100 ideas. The assumption is that brainstorming is a skill that gets better with practice. The company has figured out how to teach people to be better brainstormers and what to avoid that would kill a brainstorm.

If brainstorming gets people dreaming, then rapid prototyping gets them doing. "Prototyping is the short-hand of innovation," Kelley comments, noting that a countless number of good ideas got their start from doodles, drawings, and cobbled-together models. The idea is that if a picture is worth a thousand words, then a good prototype is worth a thousand pictures. The firm's philosophy is "build to learn," a process that includes acting before you've got the answers, taking chances, stumbling a little, and, along the way, figuring out solutions to the many small problems so that eventually you have the solution to the largest one. Says Brown, "The discovery that Thomas Edison made is that you innovate by iterating quickly, by having lots of prototypes. Prototyping allows you to learn from risks almost immediately." Adds Steelcase's Hackett, "You get a sense of the performance range of a product that teaches you more about the idea than a thousand hours spent intellectualizing it." Or, as an IDEO slogan puts it, "Fail often to succeed sooner."

Kelley tells a story that illustrates the companywide willingness to "fail forward." An employee came back from his first-ever ski trip and boasted to his team at its Monday morning meeting that he had skied for three days and never fallen down. "He expected them to pat him on the back. Instead, people heckled him, saying, "If you didn't fall down, you never pushed the envelope. You established a comfort zone and stayed in it." The lesson: You can get very good at the old status quo, but the state of the art moves on and eventually you lapse into obscurity. What fuels the creativity engine is the ingrained belief that ideas are not meant to be hoarded. IDEO spends a lot of time figuring out how to share knowledge across the company, among the managing partners, and out to the companies with whom it works. "Some organizations rely on big databases to disseminate information," says Brown. "We disseminate our knowledge through stories." Storytelling isn't limited to routine Monday morning meetings; Brown estimates that at the quarterly roundtables among IDEO's 20-odd studio heads worldwide, half the time is dedicated to sharing stories about projects or the best business practices. "People hold stories in their heads better than other forms of information," he says.

There are also Friday afternoon show-and-tell sessions to which everyone is invited, characterized by the sharing of a team's work at different phases in its projects. These meetings are marked by emptying the Tech Box, a huge filing cabinet filled with high-tech toys that aid in the communication of new concepts. "It's a way of physically manifesting the latest ideas, the things we could use in day-to-day work," explains Kelley. Many of IDEO's regular clients now have either physical or virtual Tech Boxes of their own.

Tech Boxes, storytelling, visualization, and brainstorming were at the heart of the company's development of a more inviting and efficient emergency room at the DePaul Health Center. "We were missing radical creativity," says Health Center President Bob Porter. "IDEO's methodology helped us create a dramatically different approach to how we treat our patients."

What keeps the design firm's tools honed is the philosophy that everything can be improved. "The theory IDEO espouses is that regardless of the category you compete in or the products you've had for long cycles, there are always better ways to innovate those products so users have a better experience and greater enjoyment of them," says Steelcase's Hackett, who saw IDEO take whiteboards and flip charts, a category that "didn't seem to have a real future of change," and come up with a portable and erasable writing surface called a Huddleboard Marker Board—"a conference room on-the-go, helping knowledge workers huddle together in impromptu meetings anywhere."

IDEO is teaching companies how to adapt their processes to achieve their own innovation goals. "The notion of being a strategic partner in innovation services is genuinely new," says Tom Peters, author of *In Search of Excellence*. "I don't know of anyone else as focused on transferring their own design knowledge and processes to other organizations. And I don't know of any organization that couldn't benefit from IDEO-ing itself."

Six Ways to Kill a Brainstormer:
- *The boss gets to speak first.* If the boss gets first crack, then he or she's going to set the agenda and the boundaries, and your brainstormer is immediately limited.
- *Everybody gets a turn.* Going clockwise around the room may be democratic, but it's not a brainstormer.
- *Experts only, please.* Don't be an "expert" snob. Bring in someone from manufacturing who knows how to build things. Invite a customer service rep with lots of field experience. They may not have the "right" degrees, but they just might have the insight you need.

- *Do it off-site*. While off-site brainstorming sessions are fine, you want to foster the buzz of creativity so that it blows through your offices as regularly as a breeze at the beach.
- *No silly stuff*. It's hard to overestimate what flights of fancy do for a team. They remind everybody that brainstormers aren't like regular work, that anything goes and that you can have a lot of fun while you solve the problems.
- *Write everything down*. Taking notes shifts your focus to the wrong side of your brain. It's like trying to dance and type on your laptop at the same time. Sketch all you want, doodle to your heart's delight, but leave the note taking to the designated note taker.

NOTES

INTRODUCTION: THE CALL FOR A NEW, SMARTER AGENCY ARCHITECTURE

1. Howell Raines, *Fly Fishing through the Midlife Crisis* (New York: Anchor Books, Doubleday, 1998), p. 30.
2. There is evidence that truly creative ads are much more likely to be effective than ads not honored by leading award show juries. See Leo Burnett study press release, 2002.

CHAPTER 1. AGENCY ARCHITECTURE: GETTING IT RIGHT FROM THE BEGINNING

1. Roger Menard, *My Side of the River* (Hensonville, NY: Black Dome Press, 2002), p. 87.
2. Adam Morgan, *Eating the Big Fish: How Challenger Brands Can Compete against Brand Leaders* (New York: John Wiley & Sons, 1999), and Sam Hill, *Sixty Trends in Sixty Minutes* (New York: John Wiley & Sons, 2002).
3. See Jonathan Bond and Richard Kirshenbaum, *Under the Radar* (New York: John Wiley & Sons, 1998).

CHAPTER 2. THE PITCH: MATCHING THE HATCH AND DECIDING WHAT WOULD MAKE THE CLIENT BITE DOWN ON YOUR LURE

1. Sid Evans, *The Trout Fisher's Almanac* (New York: The Atlantic Monthly Press, 1992), p. 66.
2. Peppers went on to head a brand strategy consulting firm, Peppers & Rogers Group, in Norwalk, Connecticut. He and his partner, Martha Rogers, applied the term "1-to-1 marketing"

to refer to the Web's unique ability to target individual consumers.

CHAPTER 3. CREATIVE DEPARTMENT: HOW LONG CAN IT SURVIVE AS IDEA CENTRAL?

1. Roger Traver, *Trout Madness* (New York: Simon & Schuster, 1979), p. 25.

2. Euro RSCG MVBMS defines *Creative Business Idea*™ (CBI), as an "idea that combines creative and strategy in new ways; that arises from and influences business strategy, not just communications strategy; that leads to innovative execution across traditional and new media, and indeed, brilliant execution beyond traditional and new media; that delivers breakthrough solutions and industry firsts that influence the nature of business itself; and that results in profitable innovation, transformed marketplaces/marketspaces, and new ways to maximize relationships between consumers and brands." (Source: Agency New Business Proposal, 2002.)

3. MVBMS Euro RSCG new business proposal, 2002.

4. Saatchi & Saatchi sponsors an award for Innovation in Communication. The award, which comes with a $50,000 cash prize, recognizes "outstanding innovative thinking" that improves communication. Oddly, it recognizes breakthrough thinking of outsiders, not employees of the agency. Winners include a New Zealand company that devised a way to help the visually impaired and a British company that invented a touch-sensitive, electrically conductive composite.

5. Roper Reports, 2000.

6. Communicus Tracking Study, September 2000 and July 2001, summarized by the agency.

7. *Effies 2002 Fallon*, a publication of Fallon University, Fallon Worldwide.

8. Allison-Fischer Image Barometer, 2001.

9. Autodata, 10/26/2001.

10. *Campaign* Special Report, "Media-Neutral Planning," November 8, 2002.

CHAPTER 4. MEDIA DEPARTMENT: CAN IT REPLACE CREATIVE AS THE PRIMARY SOURCE FOR BRAND-BUILDING IDEAS?

1. Tom Meade, *Essential Fly Fishing* (New York: The Lyons Press, 1994), p. 52.

2. See also Ken Sacharin, *Attention: How to Interrupt, Yell, Whisper, and Touch Consumers* (New York: John Wiley & Sons, 2001).

3. See Jonathan Bond and Richard Kirshenbaum, *Under the Radar: Talking to Today's Cynical Consumer* (New York: John Wiley & Sons, 1998).

4. *Campaign* Special Report, "Media-Neutral Planning," November 8, 2002, p. 12.

5. *Campaign* Special Report, "Media-Neutral Planning," November 8, 2002, p. 10.

CHAPTER 5. THE INTERNET AND THE AGENCY

1. David Whitlock, *Sports Afield* article, reprinted in *Trout Fisher's Almanac*, Sid Evans, ed. (New York: The Atlantic Monthly Press, 1997)., p. 23.

CHAPTER 6. PRIORITIZING STRATEGIC PLANNING

1. Roger Menard, *My Side of the River* (Hensonville, NY: Black Dome Press, 2002), p. 101.

2. Jon Steel, *Truth, Lies and Advertising: The Art of Account Planning* (New York: John Wiley & Sons, 1998), p. xv.

3. For more on Schmetterer's efforts to turn Euro RSCG into a home for great creative business ideas, see his book *Leap! A Revolution in Creative Business Strategy* (New York: John Wiley & Sons, 2003).

4. Steel, *Truth, Lies and Advertising: The Art of Account Planning,* p. 50.

5. *Campaign* Special Report, "Media-Neutral Planning," November 8, 2002, p. 4.

CHAPTER 7. GROWING YOUR AGENCY

1. David Whitlock, *Sports Afield* article, reprinted in *Trout Fisher's Almanac,* Sid Evans, ed. (New York: The Atlantic Monthly Press, 1997)., p. 23.

2. Mary Wells Lawrence, *A Big Life (in advertising)* (New York: Knopf, 2002), p. 48.

CHAPTER 8. SMART OWNERSHIP PRINCIPLES

1. John Gierach, *Trout Bum* (New York: Simon & Schuster, 1986), p. 25.

2. John M. Anderson is an attorney specializing in advertising law with Heller Ehrman White & McAuliffe, San Francisco.

CHAPTER 9. INTEGRATING AND REFOCUSING THE AGENCY NETWORK

1. Verlyn Kinkenborg, *Sports Afield* article, reprinted in *Trout Fisher's Almanac,* Sid Evans, ed. (New York: The Atlantic Monthly Press, 1997)., p. 270.

2. Volvo is the exception. It remains with Messner, part of Euro RSCG.

3. Except for Cadillac, which remains at Publicis's D'Arcy, Saturn at Omnicom's Goodby, and Oldsmobile at Publicis's Leo Burnett.

4. See Jean-Marie Dru, *Disruption: Overturning Conventions and Shaking Up the Marketplace* (New York: John Wiley & Sons, 1996).

5. See Jean-Marie Dru, *Beyond Disruption: Changing the Rules in the Marketplace* (New York: John Wiley & Sons, 2002).

6. Agnieszka Winkler, *Warp Speed Branding: The Impact of Technology on Marketing* (New York: John Wiley & Sons, 1999), p. 84.

CHAPTER 10. THE FUTURE

1. Roger Menard, *My Side of the River* (Hensonville, NY: Black Dome Press, 2002), p. 19.

2. Sergio Zyman, *The End of Marketing as We Know It* (New York: John Wiley & Sons, 2000), and *The End of Advertising as We Know It* (New York: John Wiley & Sons, 2002).

3. Roger Menard, *My Side of the River* (Hensonville, NY: Black Dome Press, 2002), p. 139.

APPENDIX A: ADVERTISING'S INVISIBLE VALUES

1. This speech was delivered to "Solutions '95, The First National Conference on Agency Financial Management and Client Compensation," Waldorf Astoria, New York, March 6, 1995. It is reprinted here by the kind permission of Sir Martin Sorrell.

APPENDIX B: A BIG FUTURE FOR BIG IDEAS

1. Excerpts from an address to the 2002 Clio Awards, Miami. Reprinted by the kind permission of the author.

APPENDIX C: THE IDEO DIFFERENCE

1. Reprinted with permission from Catherine Fredman and *Hemispheres: The Magazine of United Airlines*. This article first appeared in the August 2002 issue of *Hemispheres*.

ACKNOWLEDGMENTS

This book was made possible by the generous time and ideas provided by my many friends in the advertising industry—some quoted in these pages and some not. These include, but are by no means limited to: Michael Agate, John Anderson, Doug Atkin, David Bell, Jonathan Bond, Matt Bryant, Nick Brien, Tony Bucci, Lee Clow, John Colasanti, Jim Crimmins, Michael Donahue, John Drake, Jean-Marie Dru, Pat Fallon, Irv Fish, Neil French, Jeff Goodby, Barrie Hedge, Sam Hill, Brian Hurley, Jonathan Kamen, Rick Kurnit, Harold Levine, Bob Molineaux, Janet Northen, Millie Olson, Dean Proctor, MT Rainey, Keith Reinhard, Geoffrey Roche, Rosemarie Ryan, Bob Schmetterer, Bob Schmidt, Fred Senn, Rob Siltanen, Sir Martin Sorrell, Jon Steel, Jack Supple, Rishad Tobaccowala, Bill Tragos, Graham Warsop, Jay Waters, Ben Wiener, and Tracy Wong. Obviously, in such a book I'm drawing on 20 years' writing about, lecturing on, observing, and consulting with the advertising industry, and all the wisdom of my agency, client, and publishing associates who patiently taught me about advertising—going back to 1985 when I became the charter client of Angotti Thomas Hedge in New York and Barrie Hedge took me to breakfast to explain how a marketing plan is put together. And I am also grateful to my friends and former associates from *Adweek* who through their daily and weekly reports tell us so much about the industry—and who want it to thrive as much as I do.

I would like to give special thanks to Mark Dacey at VNU, Business Media to whom I report as head of the Clio Awards, who has generously supported this project, and to my editor at Wiley, Airié Stuart, who embraced this book from day one, as well as her associates Jessie Noyes, Emily Conway, Michelle Patterson, Linda Witzling, and publisher Larry Alexander as well as to Christine Furry of North Market Street Graphics who copyedited it. Any book aimed at such a narrow audience as this one is not destined to be a huge commercial success—but the Wiley team afforded it the same support they give all the books in the *Adweek* and *Brandweek* books series.

Special thanks to my new friend, Bob White of Whitefish Studios in Marine, Minnesota. As soon as we were introduced (by famed writer and fisherman Nick Lyons), Bob showed enthusiasm for helping me with illustrations—both for the cover and for the chapter headings. Also to my longtime fishing guide in Aspen, Colorado, Jeff Pogliano, who has shown me that sometimes you catch more fish when it's snowing than when it's sunny—perhaps a life lesson for all of us.

Finally, I would like to thank my wife, Eileen, and stepson, Nicholas, for their patience in letting me "disappear" as a husband and stepfather for most of six months while I reported and wrote this book. And thanks to my son, Christopher, for our many shared moments on waters in the United States and overseas, first when he was growing up and I was the teacher—and later when he became an expert fly fisherman and I became his student. He has taught me about casting for fish, and much, much more. And finally, to my late mother, novelist Diana Gaines Jaffe, who gave me a love of books and of writing.

INDEX